CELPIP

focus

READING and WRITING

CELPIP Focus: Reading and Writing

In response to ongoing research and development, changes may occasionally be made to the CELPIP Test. There may be short periods of time when study materials do not exactly match the current official test format, and content may be updated to match changes to the CELPIP Test without prior notice. Check celpip.ca for any updates to the CELPIP Test.

Paragon Testing Enterprises, Vancouver, British Columbia, Canada

First Printing: January 2017
Second Printing: November 2017
Third Printing: January 2019
Fourth Printing: October 2019

ISBN 978-1-988047-13-3

CONTENTS

The CELPIP Test   iv

How to Use This Book   iv

The Reading Test

    Unit 1   Overview of the Reading Test   1

    Unit 2   Reading Correspondence   6

    Unit 3   Reading to Apply a Diagram   16

    Unit 4   Reading for Information   26

    Unit 5   Reading for Viewpoints   36

The Writing Test

    Unit 6   Overview of the Writing Test   48

    Unit 7   Writing an Email   52

    Unit 8   Responding to Survey Questions   80

Answer Key   102

The CELPIP Test

About the CELPIP Test

The Canadian English Language Proficiency Index Program (CELPIP) is a computer-delivered general English language test administered by Paragon Testing Enterprises, a subsidiary of The University of British Columbia. The CELPIP Test measures how well test takers can communicate in English in a variety of social, workplace, community, and daily life situations. The format and scoring of the test are referenced to the Canadian Language Benchmarks (CLB).

The CELPIP Test is offered in two versions. This chart summarizes the main features of each version.

CELPIP – General Test			CELPIP – General LS Test		
✓ Four-skills test			✓ Two-skills test		
✓ About 3 hours			✓ About 1 hour 10 minutes		
Listening	6 parts*	47–55 minutes	**Listening**	6 parts	47–55 minutes
Reading	4 parts*	55–60 minutes	**Speaking**	8 tasks	15–20 minutes
Writing	2 tasks	53–60 minutes			
Speaking	8 tasks	15–20 minutes			

* There may be additional unscored items in the Listening and/or Reading tests which are used for research and development purposes. See celpip.ca for more information.

Tip Doing a CELPIP Practice Test is a great way to familiarize yourself with test features and get ready for your test day. You can access free practice test questions and purchase practice tests at celpip.ca.

How to Use This Book

This book is divided into two modules, Reading and Writing. Each unit within a module is independent of the others, so you can do them in any order. Since the skills get harder to master as you work through the module, it is easier to start at the beginning of the module and work through the units in order.

Features

Look for the icons shown below to quickly locate specific features.

 READING SKILLS:
These skills help you deal with challenging readings during the Reading Test.

 WRITING SKILLS:
These skills help you complete your Writing tasks. teaches

 ACTIVITY:
These are practice opportunities for the skill you are learning. Answers, some with explanations, are provided in the Answer Key.

 TIP:
These are important tips and strategies to improve performance on the test.

 TIME MANAGEMENT:
These give specific guidance on how to manage your time for one Reading part or Writing task.

The Modules

The Reading Module

- The format of the four parts of the Reading Test is explained.
- The different kinds of questions found on the Reading Test are discussed.
- Each part of the Reading Test has a separate unit.
- An infographic shows key computer navigation features for the Reading Test.
- Infographics for each test part highlight the key elements and challenges.

The Writing Module

- An overview of the test component explains the format of the Writing Test and gives information about scoring.
- Each task of the Writing Test has a separate unit.
- An infographic shows key computer navigation features for the Writing Test.
- Infographics for each task highlight the key elements and challenges.
- Sample responses have been provided for most Writing tasks.
- Writing tasks from CELPIP Tests are presented as they look on the test screen.

Each unit focuses on key language skills and essential test-taking strategies. A complete Answer Key is included, with explanations for some activities. The scoring checklist will help you assess your Writing responses.

For Instructors

Use this book to build your own CELPIP test preparation course. The activities here are best suited to self-study, but many can be adapted for working in groups of two or more. Here are a few suggestions to get you started:

- Students can work in pairs to complete an activity.
- Students can complete an activity alone and discuss their answers in small groups.
- After completing an exercise, students can exchange books and mark each other's answers.
- Students can provide feedback on each other's Writing responses using the writing checklists in Units 7 and 8.
- Students can work in small groups to study one skill in a unit and present it to the class.

Accessing Updates

Please periodically check the link below for updates to this book.

Online Resource: https://www.celpip.ca/celpip-focus-rw/

UNIT 1

Overview of the Reading Test

LEARNING FOCUS

- Format of the Reading Test
- Understanding question format
- Identifying question types
- Improving your reading

The CELPIP-General Reading Test includes a variety of texts found in everyday life. This includes email messages, short articles, diagrams, and website postings. You will be required to locate information, infer meaning, identify main points and important details, and perform other reading tasks as you complete each part of the test.

In this unit, you will become familiar with the overall format and the different types of questions you will find on the Reading Test. Knowing what to expect on the Reading Test can make a big difference in your performance.

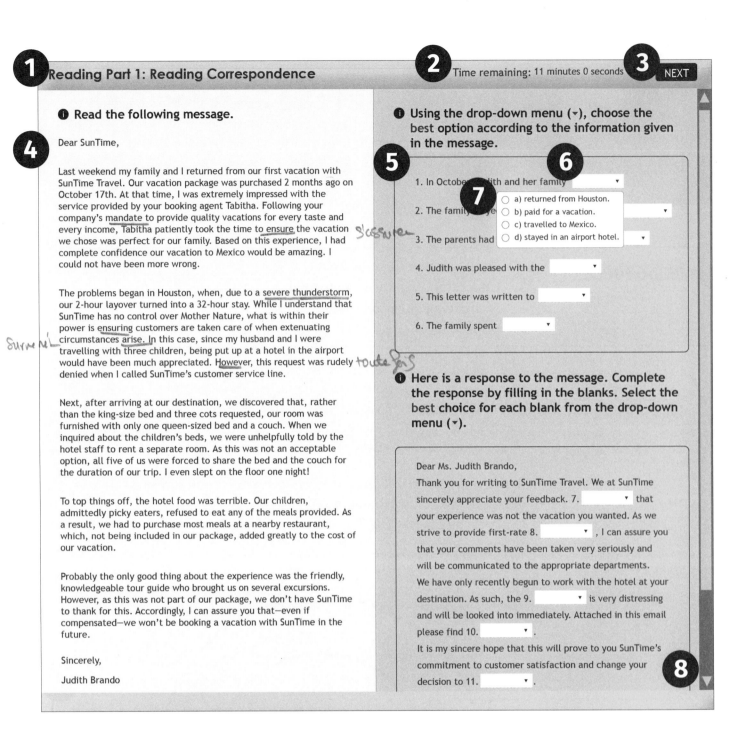

Dear SunTime,

Last weekend my family and I returned from our first vacation with SunTime Travel. Our vacation package was purchased 2 months ago on October 17th. At that time, I was extremely impressed with the service provided by your booking agent Tabitha. Following your company's mandate to provide quality vacations for every taste and every income, Tabitha patiently took the time to ensure the vacation we chose was perfect for our family. Based on this experience, I had complete confidence our vacation to Mexico would be amazing. I could not have been more wrong.

The problems began in Houston, when, due to a severe thunderstorm, our 2-hour layover turned into a 32-hour stay. While I understand that SunTime has no control over Mother Nature, what is within their power is ensuring customers are taken care of when extenuating circumstances arise. In this case, since my husband and I were travelling with three children, being put up at a hotel in the airport would have been much appreciated. However, this request was rudely denied when I called SunTime's customer service line.

Next, after arriving at our destination, we discovered that, rather than the king-size bed and three cots requested, our room was furnished with only one queen-sized bed and a couch. When we inquired about the children's beds, we were unhelpfully told by the hotel staff to rent a separate room. As this was not an acceptable option, all five of us were forced to share the bed and the couch for the duration of our trip. I even slept on the floor one night!

To top things off, the hotel food was terrible. Our children, admittedly picky eaters, refused to eat any of the meals provided. As a result, we had to purchase most meals at a nearby restaurant, which, not being included in our package, added greatly to the cost of our vacation.

Probably the only good thing about the experience was the friendly, knowledgeable tour guide who brought us on several excursions. However, as this was not part of our package, we don't have SunTime to thank for this. Accordingly, I can assure you that—even if compensated—we won't be booking a vacation with SunTime in the future.

Sincerely,

Judith Brando

Using the drop-down menu (▾), choose the best option according to the information given in the message.

1. In October, Judith and her family ___ ▾
   ○ a) returned from Houston.
   ○ b) paid for a vacation.
   ○ c) travelled to Mexico.
   ○ d) stayed in an airport hotel.

2. The family ___ ▾

3. The parents had ___ ▾

4. Judith was pleased with the ___ ▾

5. This letter was written to ___ ▾

6. The family spent ___ ▾

Here is a response to the message. Complete the response by filling in the blanks. Select the best choice for each blank from the drop-down menu (▾).

Dear Ms. Judith Brando,

Thank you for writing to SunTime Travel. We at SunTime sincerely appreciate your feedback. 7. ___ ▾ that your experience was not the vacation you wanted. As we strive to provide first-rate 8. ___ ▾ , I can assure you that your comments have been taken very seriously and will be communicated to the appropriate departments.

We have only recently begun to work with the hotel at your destination. As such, the 9. ___ ▾ is very distressing and will be looked into immediately. Attached in this email please find 10. ___ ▾ .

It is my sincere hope that this will prove to you SunTime's commitment to customer satisfaction and change your decision to 11. ___ ▾ .

---

① Title reminds you where you are in test.

② Countdown timer shows how much time you have left for this page. When timer reaches zero, test will move to next part.

③ Use NEXT button to move to next part before timer reaches zero. You cannot move back.

④ Main reading is always on left side.

⑤ One or two answer areas are always on right side.

⑥ Click on arrow to see answer choices.

⑦ Click on circle to select best answer. Change answers as many times as you like.

⑧ Scroll to move up or down and see more text.

Format of the Reading Test

There are four main parts in the Reading Test. You will also have one short practice task to help familiarize you with the format of the text and timer. There may be additional unscored items which are used for research and development purposes. You will have about one hour to complete the Reading Test. This test is computer scored and it gets more difficult as you work through it.

Each reading screen has the same basic format.

READING PART	READING PASSAGES	TASKS
Practice Task	• Short passage of text	• Practice reading and answering a question.
Reading Correspondence	• Long message • Short response	• Answer 6 questions about the long message. • Fill in 5 blanks in the short response.
Reading to Apply a Diagram	• Diagram • Message	• Fill in 5 blanks in the message by referring to the diagram. • Answer 3 comprehension questions.
Reading for Information	• Long passage	• Read a 4-paragraph passage and 9 statements. Select which paragraph (if any) each statement comes from.
Reading for Viewpoints	• Website posting • Reader's comment	• Complete 5 sentences about the website posting. • Fill in 5 blanks in the reader's comment.
Unscored Items	• Same format as one of the above	• These will be the same as one of the above.
TOTAL TIME		**About 1 hour**

Understanding Question Format

All questions that may appear on the Reading Test are multiple choice, and there are four different styles, shown below.

1) **Sentence-Completion Questions**
   Choose among four ways of completing a single sentence.

1. Tom was missing from work in September because he _____ ▾

2. After returning to work, To|

   ○ a) went on a month-long vacation.
   ○ b) travelled to his home country.
   ○ c) visited his sister in Nova Scotia.
   ○ d) stayed at a destination resort.

3. The manager of the store h|

2) **Text-Completion Questions**
   Fill in the blanks in a text by selecting from four multiple choice answers.

I am glad you brought this to my attention. This is an issue that

7. _____ ▾ , and I will have my team deal with it immediately.

   ○ a) is important to fix at once   roblem, please message me
   ○ b) has happened twice before   . I will be away 8. _____ ▾ ,
   ○ c) I thought we had resolved   ll me on my phone instead of
   ○ d) others have found as well

3) **WH Questions**

Answer questions that begin with words like what, when, where, and why.

1. What is the purpose of the email?

2. The reply from the company

3. After reading the email, the

- ○ a) To ask about extra costs
- ○ b) To provide more information
- ○ c) To include additional guests
- ○ d) To confirm a reservation

4) **Matching Questions**

Match a statement to one of four paragraphs, identified as A, B, C, and D. If the statement does not match any of the paragraphs, choose E. This style appears in Reading Part 3 only.

ⓘ **Decide which paragraph, A to D, has the information given in each statement below. Select E if the information is not given in any of the paragraphs.**

- ○ A
- ○ B
- ○ C
- ○ D
- ○ E

1. In 2013, the forestry industry in British Columbia made over $15 billion in revenue.

2. Canada implemented many policies that limited the amount of logging, in order to prevent deforestation.

Identifying Question Types

Questions for the Reading Test can be grouped into three types:

1. General Meaning	2. Specific Details	3. Inference
• These are questions that focus on understanding the overall idea in a text. • You may be asked to identify the topic, theme, or main idea of a reading passage.	• These are questions that focus on understanding specific details in a text. • You may be asked to identify key details, supporting details, opinions, or examples.	• These are questions that focus on drawing conclusions and making assumptions based on information in a text. • You may be asked to identify implicit information, including an author's purpose, tone, or attitude.

globale

Activity 1

Read the sample text from Reading Part 1 on page 2, and answer the questions below. Check your answers in the Answer Key.

1. In October, Judith and her family
   a) returned from Houston.
   b) paid for a vacation.
   c) travelled to Mexico.
   d) stayed in an airport hotel.

2. This message was written to
   a) express dissatisfaction.
   b) provide a suggestion.
   c) request a refund.
   d) show appreciation.

3. To make up for her bad experience with the company, Judith wants SunTime to
   a) book her vacation for next year.
   b) advise her about other good travel destinations with SunTime.
   c) apologize and refund some or all of her travel expenses.
   d) tell her the name of the tour guide.

Activity 2

Identify the question type for each question on the previous page. Check your answers and read the explanations provided in the Answer Key to understand how to identify question types.

Question Number	Question Type
1	specific details ✓
2	general meaning ✓
3	Inference ✓

Improving Your Reading

In preparing for the Reading Test, there are various ways to improve your skills. Try to set aside some time each day, even if it's only a few minutes, to read something new. To build a well-rounded vocabulary, try to expose yourself to different types of reading material, such as newspapers, magazines, journals, online articles, sports commentary, and novels. The Canadian Broadcasting Corporation (CBC) website is a great place to start. Most importantly, read things you're interested in—this will make your reading practice much more enjoyable, and you may learn new words and phrases more easily.

LEARNING FOCUS

- Reading skills
- Previewing
- Skimming
- Scanning

Reading Part 1: Reading Correspondence starts with a personal letter or email. This is followed by a set of comprehension questions and a short response message with text-completion questions. To answer the questions, you need to understand the general meaning of the original message, locate specific details, and relate the response to the original message. You may need to infer knowledge based on your reading of the initial message.

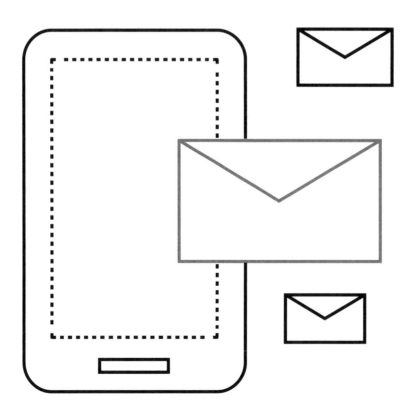

1 **ⓘ Read the following message.**

Hi Janice,

I would like to apply for a leave of absence for the month of December. I know that's a very busy time for us in the store, and it will leave you in a difficult position since I am the chief buyer. I wouldn't ask except that it's important.

Lately I've been feeling very tired and not at all like myself. I went to the doctor and he said that I'm experiencing stress and that I must take time off. He said I have to do that now, before it gets any worse. I love my job, but he says stress can happen because of being too busy for too long. Well, that does describe me all right!

Fortunately, we've already interviewed some promising new staff members to help during the busy Christmas season. Perhaps they *new - être* could start work soon, and I can help train them during the next two weeks before I'm off. I'm sure we'll have a good balance of experienced staff and new sales staff to see us through the busy period.

I've been ordering stock this month, as usual, so that we are fully prepared for Christmas shoppers. I think it's unlikely that more shoe orders will need to be made in December, unless there are special orders for occasions such as weddings. That's usually your area of expertise anyway. *en lout cas -* *souvent*

If you recall, last summer you asked me to prepare a procedures manual for all store staff. I did this, and the permanent staff have given me feedback. I've made all the changes. It explains everything, such as store policies, breaks and time off, shifts, cash register procedures and problems, and chain of command. I think this will help new staff members learn what to do in their job.

David and I have made arrangements to spend the month in Florida. Hopefully the weather will be warm and sunny. The cottage we've *chalet* rented is right on the beach and a bit isolated. I'm glad about that because we want to rest, not get caught up in a busy social circle.

Again, I'm sorry for the inconvenience, but I have no choice.

Thanks,

Tracey

---

2 **ⓘ Using the drop-down menu (▾), choose the best option according to the information given in the message.**

3

1. Who is Tracey writing to? [▾]

     ○ a) a coworker
     ○ b) a doctor
     ○ c) her friend
     ○ d) her manager

2. Which item would the sto[...] [▾]

3. Why is Tracey worried ab[...] r off? [▾]

4. Tracey is going to Florida to [▾]

5. Which statement best describes Tracey? [▾]

6. Why does Tracey mention the manual? [▾]

ⓘ Here is a response to the message. Complete the response by filling in the blanks. Select the best choice for each blank from the drop-down menu (▾).

4

Hi Tracey,

I've noticed that you haven't seemed yourself lately, and I've been worried. I'm glad you are 7. [▾]. But it will be difficult getting through 8. [▾] without you!

5

I'm wondering if you ordered enough of product number BL-4829. This item was very popular last winter, so I think it 9. [▾] Maybe you could show me how to reorder, so I can be prepared. Overall, I agree that 10. [▾].

As you say, we have some good temporary staff members starting soon. I'll contact them to see if they can begin work next Monday. You and I can do the training together. I'm sure 11. [▾] will be useful when you're not here.

I hope the break in December does you good!

Janice

---

①   Main passage is email.

②   There are eleven questions in total.

③   First six questions refer to main passage.

④   Second passage is response to main passage.

⑤   There are five text-completion questions for short response.

Reading Skills

There are three essential reading skills that will help you complete the Reading Test within the given time.

PREVIEWING: Glance quickly at the overall structure of the screen, identify the various sections, and check how long you have to answer the questions.

SKIMMING: Look over the main text quickly to identify the topic, and get a general idea of the content by reading over the first sentence of each paragraph.

SCANNING: Quickly locate the information you need to answer the question.

You should spend about 1–2 minutes previewing and skimming a passage as soon as it comes onscreen, before looking at the questions. It is not necessary to read the entire text to find the information you need. Skimming the text first will give you a general idea of where to look for specific details when you are answering the questions.

Previewing

When each test part begins, start by previewing the screen to check format and timing.

- Determine how long you have to complete this part of the test.
- Identify how many sections there are.
- Check how many questions there are.

Activity 1

Without looking back at the reading on page 7, answer the following questions:

1. How long do you have to complete Reading Part 1?

2. How many sections are there?

3. How many questions are there?

4. Roughly how long do you have to answer each question?

Skimming

Skimming is a type of speed-reading; you need to quickly look over the text to understand how the passage is organized and identify the topic of each paragraph. Follow these steps when you skim a passage:

- Read the first sentence or two of each paragraph; the main idea of a paragraph is often introduced here.
- Spend a little more time on the first paragraph; the topic will be introduced here.
- Make note of words and phrases that are repeated; these may be key words in the test questions.

Activity 2A

Reading Part 1 is formatted as a personal message and response. Read the Greeting, Sign-off, and first sentence of each paragraph in the reading on page 7 and answer the questions below. These questions will help guide your reading as you go through this part.

1. Who is the writer? _Tracey_ ✓

2. Who is the recipient? _Janice_ ✓

3. Paragraph 1:
   a) Tracey is requesting 1 month off work at the end of the year.
   b) Tracey wants to leave work for 2 months, beginning next month.
   c) Tracey has the right to ask for a leave of absence for a month.
   d) Tracey needs to leave work early today as she has an errand to run.

4. Paragraph 2:
   a) Tracey is explaining why she's tired of her current position.
   b) Tracey is informing the reader about how tired she is today.
   c) Tracey is giving reasons for her request for a leave of absence.
   d) Tracey is giving reasons why she prefers working by herself.

5. Paragraph 3:
   a) Tracey is informing the reader of the promises made by new staff.
   b) Tracey is finished interviewing new staff for Christmas.
   c) Tracey is busy during Christmas and can't do more interviews.
   d) Tracey is informing the reader of the upcoming interviews.

6. Paragraph 4:
   a) They will need more stock for December.
   b) Stock is already ordered for Christmas.
   c) As usual, shoppers are ready for Christmas.
   d) She has prepared stock for all occasions.

7. Paragraph 5:
   a) The manual for all store staff is ready.
   b) Tracey cannot recall what she did last summer.
   c) Tracey is waiting for feedback about the manual.
   d) Tracey had asked her manager for feedback last summer.

8. Paragraph 6:
   a) Tracey will arrange to stay in Florida soon.
   b) Tracey will be alone in Florida for 30 days.
   c) Tracey has asked David to make arrangements.
   d) Tracey has planned a trip for two to Florida.

9. What is the relationship between the writer and the recipient? _Employee / Manager_

10. What is the main purpose of the email? _informing her manager that Tracey need a month of leave._

9

Activity 2B

When we skim a passage, we don't read every word. We look over the text quickly, skipping over words that we don't understand, and focusing on general meaning. In this activity, parts of the message have been blacked out, but you can still understand the main points by skimming the key words and phrases that are visible.

Skim the following email and answer the questions based on the key words and phrases visible in the message. Then read the explanations in the Answer Key.

> ▮ glad to hear ▮▮▮▮▮ holiday! ▮▮▮▮▮
>
> ▮▮▮▮ difference between motels and hotels, ▮▮ motels ▮▮▮▮▮ rooms ▮
> ▮▮▮▮▮▮▮ ground floor ▮▮▮ doors ▮▮▮▮▮ to the
> parking lot. Hotels, ▮▮▮▮ have several floors ▮▮▮▮▮▮
> underground parking ▮▮▮▮▮▮▮▮
> prefer a motel ▮▮▮▮▮▮▮ on the ground floor, ▮▮▮
> instant exit ▮▮▮▮ emergency. ▮▮▮▮ forget something ▮▮▮▮ back ▮
> car ▮▮
>
> ▮▮▮ do some research ▮▮▮▮▮▮ where to stay. ▮▮▮▮
> ▮▮▮▮▮▮▮ websites ▮▮ travel guides ▮
> ▮▮▮▮▮▮▮▮▮▮
> ▮▮▮▮ written reviews ▮▮▮▮▮▮▮
> ▮▮▮▮▮▮▮▮▮▮
> ▮▮▮▮▮▮▮▮▮▮
> complaining ▮▮▮▮ bedbugs ▮ unclean bathrooms! ▮▮▮▮ managers ▮▮
> ▮▮▮▮ comply ▮▮▮ company's standards ▮▮▮

1. Who is going on vacation?
   a) The author of the email
   b) The recipient of the email
   c) The author and the recipient
   d) None of the above

2. In the first paragraph, the author
   a) compares hotels and motels.
   b) expresses a preference.
   c) prefers to stay in his car.
   d) both a) and b)

3. In the second paragraph, the author
   a) suggests doing some research on motels.
   b) warns against the poor condition of some motels.
   c) refers the reader to written reviews.
   d) All of the above

10

The passage you just skimmed contains 231 words, but only about one-quarter of these were visible. This demonstrates that even if you don't understand all the words, you may still be able to determine the overall meaning of a passage. The chart below shows how a high-level test taker might use the blacked-out information to determine the general idea of the passage.

The author of the passage			
compares	motels	• rooms on ground floor • doors to the parking lot	
	hotels	• several floors • underground parking	
expresses a preference	motels	• ground floor • instant exit • easy access to car	
suggests	researching	• websites • travel guides • written reviews	
warns against	badly managed hotels	• complaints • bed bugs • unclean bathrooms • not meeting company standards	

Scanning

Scanning will help you locate specific details in the original message to complete the response and to answer the questions. The ability to recognize paraphrases can help with this. When a piece of text is paraphrased, different words are used to express the same meaning. For example, a paraphrase of "locate specific words" is "find particular terms." The meaning remains the same, but different words—synonyms—have been used.

Since paraphrasing is often used in answer choices, try to notice synonyms or rephrased terms as you scan the text. Follow these steps to develop your scanning skills:

- Identify the information you need to find (read the question!).
- Briefly imagine what the information will look like (will it be a name, a number, a date, a phrase?).
- Skim the article to determine where the information might be (which paragraph?).
- Scan the target paragraph, and then read any sentences that might have the answer (focus on a specific chunk of text).
- Minimize time spent reading paragraphs that likely don't have the answer (stay focused).

Activity 3

Look at the question and scan the partial text to find the best answer. Look for words in the text that are synonyms or related to the words in the answer choices to help you find the answer. Then read the explanation in the Answer Key.

1. Most **motels** have
   a) a single **storey**.
   b) a small **parking lot**.
   c) too few emergency **exits**.
   d) rooms with two **doors**.

> **Motels** is definitely a key word here

> Watch for these key words, or their synonyms, in the text.

> **Floor** is mentioned frequently here; perhaps that's important.

Hi Jason,

As for the difference between motels and hotels, most motels have all of their rooms—and everything else—on the ground floor and their doors open directly to the parking lot. Hotels, on the other hand, have several floors—sometimes as many as fifty—and underground parking. I know you're travelling with your dog, so you'll probably prefer a motel. Honestly, I like motels better because if I'm on the ground floor, I've got an instant exit in the event of an emergency. And if I forget something, it's easy to run back out to my car to get it!

2. **Managers** have a lot of control over
   a) the **prices** they charge.
   b) the **services** they provide.
   c) the **quality** of their motels or hotels.
   d) the **reviews** of their motels or hotels.

> **Managers** seems to be a key word that we should be able to find in the text.

> Watch for these key words, or their synonyms, in the text.

> "**Highest quality**" in this phrase is a good hint. Maybe the answer relates to "**quality**."

You should do some research so you can decide ahead of time where to stay. This is important to do before you leave. I suggest you look at websites and in travel guides for reviews of hotels and motels. Most are rated on a five-star scale where a five-star rating means the highest quality. However, written reviews can be more helpful than star ratings because these reviews may mention things not listed on the websites or guides. I almost booked a room at a popular and respected hotel chain, but then I read some reviews complaining that they had bedbugs and unclean bathrooms! I guess some managers make sure their establishments comply with the company's standards, and some don't.

3. Marcel's **main point** is that his friend should
   a) **make some inquiries** before he leaves.
   b) consider **leaving his pet** at home.
   c) stay at a **hotel** instead of a motel.
   d) **make reservations** in advance.

> **Main point** indicates that this question is asking for the purpose here...

> Watch for these key terms, or their synonyms, in the text.

> The question states that Marcel's friend may need to **consider doing something**. There are a number of sentences phrased as **suggestions** in this paragraph, so it might be a good idea to start with these.

Often, the star rating is based on the number of amenities the hotel or motel offers. This is also something for you to consider because things like internet are usually free, but parking sometimes costs extra—you don't want to be surprised by this. Will you want breakfast included? Do you plan on swimming? You probably won't care about room service. And I know you're travelling with your dog; some motels charge a mandatory pet fee in addition to the basic room fee. Check out the written reviews, the websites, and the guides to find the hotel experience you want. And be sure to check for extra fees. Sometimes it's even a good idea to call the hotel or motel directly because this information may not be found anywhere else.

Good luck, have fun, and send me some pictures!

Marcel

Time Management
- **EMAIL:** Take up to **1 minute** to **skim** for a quick overview.
- **COMPREHENSION QUESTIONS:** Take about **45 seconds** for **each question**.
- **SHORT RESPONSE:** Spend **1 minute skimming** the text. Choose an answer for **each question** within **45 seconds**.

Test Practice

Use the skills you have learned in this unit to answer these questions from a new example of Reading Part 1.

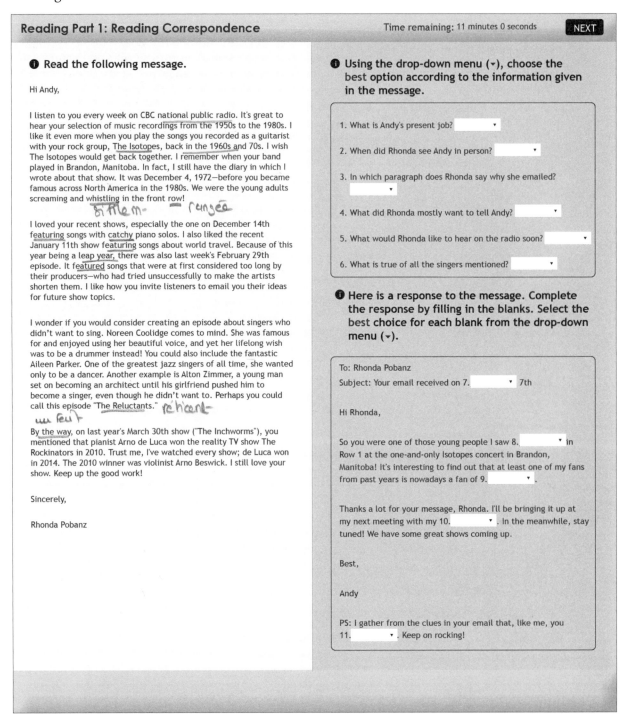

Reading Part 1: Reading Correspondence   Time remaining: 11 minutes 0 seconds   NEXT

ℹ **Read the following message.**

Hi Andy,

I listen to you every week on CBC national public radio. It's great to hear your selection of music recordings from the 1950s to the 1980s. I like it even more when you play the songs you recorded as a guitarist with your rock group, The Isotopes, back in the 1960s and 70s. I wish The Isotopes would get back together. I remember when your band played in Brandon, Manitoba. In fact, I still have the diary in which I wrote about that show. It was December 4, 1972—before you became famous across North America in the 1980s. We were the young adults screaming and whistling in the front row!

I loved your recent shows, especially the one on December 14th featuring songs with catchy piano solos. I also liked the recent January 11th show featuring songs about world travel. Because of this year being a leap year, there was also last week's February 29th episode. It featured songs that were at first considered too long by their producers—who had tried unsuccessfully to make the artists shorten them. I like how you invite listeners to email you their ideas for future show topics.

I wonder if you would consider creating an episode about singers who didn't want to sing. Noreen Coolidge comes to mind. She was famous for and enjoyed using her beautiful voice, and yet her lifelong wish was to be a drummer instead! You could also include the fantastic Aileen Parker. One of the greatest jazz singers of all time, she wanted only to be a dancer. Another example is Alton Zimmer, a young man set on becoming an architect until his girlfriend pushed him to become a singer, even though he didn't want to. Perhaps you could call this episode "The Reluctants."

By the way, on last year's March 30th show ("The Inchworms"), you mentioned that pianist Arno de Luca won the reality TV show The Rockinators in 2010. Trust me, I've watched every show; de Luca won in 2014. The 2010 winner was violinist Arno Beswick. I still love your show. Keep up the good work!

Sincerely,

Rhonda Pobanz

ℹ **Using the drop-down menu (▾), choose the best option according to the information given in the message.**

1. What is Andy's present job? [▾]

2. When did Rhonda see Andy in person? [▾]

3. In which paragraph does Rhonda say why she emailed? [▾]

4. What did Rhonda mostly want to tell Andy? [▾]

5. What would Rhonda like to hear on the radio soon? [▾]

6. What is true of all the singers mentioned? [▾]

ℹ **Here is a response to the message. Complete the response by filling in the blanks. Select the best choice for each blank from the drop-down menu (▾).**

To: Rhonda Pobanz

Subject: Your email received on 7. [▾] 7th

Hi Rhonda,

So you were one of those young people I saw 8. [▾] in Row 1 at the one-and-only Isotopes concert in Brandon, Manitoba! It's interesting to find out that at least one of my fans from past years is nowadays a fan of 9. [▾].

Thanks a lot for your message, Rhonda. I'll be bringing it up at my next meeting with my 10. [▾]. In the meanwhile, stay tuned! We have some great shows coming up.

Best,

Andy

PS: I gather from the clues in your email that, like me, you 11. [▾]. Keep on rocking!

---

1. What is Andy's present job?
   a) radio show host
   b) radio show director
   c) radio show musician
   d) radio show recorder

2. When did Rhonda see Andy in person?
   a) in the 1950s
   b) in the 1960s
   c) in the 1970s
   d) in the 1980s

3. In which paragraph does Rhonda say why she emailed?
   a) one
   b) two
   c) three
   d) four

4. What did Rhonda mostly want to tell Andy?
   a) a correction
   b) a suggestion
   c) a complaint
   d) her memories

5. What would Rhonda like to hear on the radio soon?
   a) songs recorded by unwilling singers
   b) songs with a world travel theme
   c) songs that are longer than normal
   d) songs with interesting piano solos

6. What is true of all the singers mentioned?
   a) Singing was their second career.
   b) Singing was not fun for them.
   c) They were better at something else.
   d) They wanted a different job.

7. a) December
   b) January
   c) February
   d) March

8. a) dancing to the music
   b) jumping up and down
   c) making loud noises
   d) waving your arms

9. a) The Rockinators on television
   b) live concerts by The Inchworms
   c) The Reluctants on television
   d) live concerts by The Isotopes

10. a) band members
    b) concert organizers
    c) recording engineers
    d) show producers

11. a) have travelled the world
    b) play guitar passionately
    c) sing rather unwillingly
    d) were born in the 1950s

LEARNING FOCUS

- Dealing with diagrams
- Diagram variety
- Identifying purpose and tone

Reading Part 2: Reading to Apply a Diagram features short texts in graphical format, such as brochures, websites, invoices, instruction manuals, menus, advertisements, and timetables. The accompanying email contains five blanks that must be completed using information found in the diagram. Another three questions follow the email; these questions may be phrased as full or incomplete sentences. To answer the questions, you need to locate specific information in the diagram, make connections between the diagram and the email, and understand the purpose and tone of the email.

2

Wanda's Wonderful Weddings
- Delicious vegan, nut-free, and gluten-free cheesecake, guaranteed safe for allergy requirements (send us a list of your guests' allergies to be sure!)
- Single or double layers available to serve 25 to 50 wedding guests
- Berry or fruit topping varies according to availability
- $10 per slice, including topping on each slice

Barbara's Best Bakery
- Try the traditional choice of delicious white cake professionally decorated with white fondant icing
- Decorated tastefully with fresh fragrant red roses and matching ribbon; colour can be your preference
- Two or three layers, serving 75 to 100 guests
- $8 per slice
- Keeps fresh for several weeks in the fridge

Theresa's Tastiest Treats
- Delicious layers of lemon cake joined together with unbeatable buttercream frosting
- Your choice of frosting colour or traditional white
- Fresh fruit or berry topping according to season, adds colour, creativity, and flavour
- A variety of sizes depending on your guest list
- Reasonable prices
- Your order can be customized to your preferences

Olia's Online Occasions
- Voted the most popular wedding cake of the year
- Consult us online; then we give you a taste test in your home
- Layers of alternating dark and white chocolate cake with contrasting white chocolate and dark chocolate frosting
- Decorations in a theme of your choice, such as this ocean theme, as pictured
- Prices start at $150 for a two-layer cake serving 75 guests

ⓘ Read the following email message about the diagram on the left. Complete the email by filling in the blanks. Select the best choice for each blank from the drop-down menu (▾).

3

Subject: Wedding cake
To: Janice Jackson <jjackson@walker.com>
From: Alice Morrison <amorrison@local.ca>

Hi Janice,

I need your help choosing a wedding cake. Alan says any cake will do as long as it tastes great, so he's no help. My mother put together a list of four cake possibilities. I think she even contacted each place and did a taste test!

About 10% of our guests need a gluten-free option, and 1. [____▾] would certainly be a good choice, but I think it's too unusual, even for me. The wedding is in early July, so 2. [____▾] should be readily available for a scrumptious topping for the lemon cake. *delicious*

4

However, it looks very casual compared to the beautiful cake from 3. [____▾]. That one also serves the most people. I wonder if 4. [____▾] would change the roses for strawberries, though. *pense* *attirant* That might make it even more appealing. 5. [____▾] that *theme* themed cake sure looks worth sampling!   *vaut la peine*

Please help me choose!   *d'être échantillonné*

Alice

ⓘ Using the drop-down menu (▾), choose the best option.

5

6. Alan is [____▾]

7. Alice thinks her mother [____▾]

8. Alice's choice will likely [____▾]

---

① **Main passage is diagram.**

② **Diagram could be an advertisement, brochure, menu, catalogue page, or something else.**

③ **There are eight questions in total.**

④ **There are five text-completion questions in email about diagram.**

⑤ **There are three additional questions after message.**

Dealing with Diagrams

Many different types of diagrams are used in this part of the Reading Test. Several examples appear in this textbook, but you are likely to see other types on the official test. Although there are a variety of diagrams used on the official test, there are some key strategies that can be applied to this part of the test, regardless of the type of diagram that is used. These key strategies include recognizing paraphrases and identifying purpose and tone.

> **Tip** You will often have to compare two or more pieces of information in the diagram to answer questions.

As discussed in Unit 2, the ability to identify paraphrases on the Reading Test can help you to answer questions related to specific information. There will rarely be word-to-word matches between the questions and the Reading passage itself; instead, synonyms are often used. Keeping an eye out for these will help you identify paraphrases. The activities below will help you learn to quickly find specific details in diagrams that you will need to answer questions.

Activity 1A

Find the word or phrase in the diagram on page 17 that is most similar in meaning to the words listed below. Write the word(s) in the blank. The first one has been done for you.

1. classic   __traditional__
(See Barbara's Best Bakery, point 1)

2. chosen   _____

3. inexpensive   _____

4. definite   _____

5. superior   _____

Activity 1B

Complete these sentences to test your ability to recognize the synonym pairs above.

1. I want a **classic** wedding cake, so I plan to buy from _____.

2. Since some of my guests can't eat wheat, I have to go with the only bakery that **definitely** provides allergy-free cakes: _____.

3. In my opinion, buttercream frosting is the most important part of the wedding cake—I want the cake with the **superior** frosting! I'm going with _____.

4. I read that _____'s wedding cake was **chosen** as the most popular one this year, so I'll be getting my cake from them.

5. My husband and I are really hoping for an **inexpensive** but very creative cake with fruit on top so we're buying from _____.

Activity 1C

Using the diagram on page 17, answer the following questions and include information from the diagram to support your answer. The first question has been done for you.

1. Which bakery offers options for dietary restrictions?

   <u>Wanda's Wonderful Weddings—they offer vegan, nut-free, and gluten-free options.</u>

2. What items does Barbara's Bakery use to decorate their "traditional" cakes?

   _____

3. Which bakery will decorate cakes however you like?

   _____

4. What is the name of the bakery that doesn't advertise their prices?

   _____

Activity 1D

Which bakery from the diagram is most suitable for the following couples? Write the name of the bakery on the line provided and include at least two reasons to support your choice.

1. Brian and Gloria have a very specific wedding theme in mind that they want to follow exactly—and they want the very best! They would like to choose the most popular option, as that is likely to give them the result they want, but they would like to try the cake before deciding on a bakery.

   _____

2. Kyle and Diana are having a small wedding, with only family and close friends, so their guest list is small. They have several dietary restrictions as well: Diana is vegan, and Kyle's mother is allergic to nuts.

   _____

Activity 1E

Now that you have practiced finding specific details in the diagram on page 17, read the following email and complete it by filling in the blanks. Select the best choice for each blank from the options below. Explanations have been provided in the Answer Key.

Subject: Wedding cake

To: Janice Jackson <jjackson@walker.com>

From: Alice Morrison <amorrison@local.ca>

Hi Janice,

I need your help choosing a wedding cake. Alan says any cake will do as long as it tastes great, so he's no help. My mother put together a list of four cake possibilities. I think she even contacted each place and did a taste test!

About 10% of our guests need a gluten-free option, and 1. ▾ would certainly be a good choice, but I think it's too unusual, even for me. The wedding is in early July, so 2. ▾ should be readily available for a scrumptious topping for the lemon cake. However, it looks very casual compared to the beautiful cake from 3. ▾ . That one also serves the most people. I wonder if 4. ▾ would change the roses for strawberries, though. That might make it even more appealing. 5. ▾ that themed cake sure looks worth sampling!

Please help me choose!

Alice

---

1. a) lemon cake
   b) cheesecake
   c) chocolate topping
   d) red rose topping

2. a) flavoured coffee beans
   b) chocolate frosting
   c) pretty rosebuds
   d) local strawberries

3. a) Wanda's
   b) Theresa's
   c) Barbara's
   d) Olia's

4. a) Olia's Online Occasions
   b) Theresa's Tastiest Treats
   c) Wanda's Wonderful Weddings
   d) Barbara's Best Bakery

5. a) After all,
   b) All in all,
   c) Additionally,
   d) On the other hand,

6. Alan is
   a) Alice's fiancé.
   b) Janice's husband.
   c) Alice's father.
   d) Janice's friend.

7. Alice thinks her mother
   a) has the same point of view as Alan.
   b) made some helpful cake suggestions.
   c) ought to make the decision herself.
   d) probably wants the most popular cake.

8. Alice's choice will likely
   a) be an ocean-themed wedding cake.
   b) include local strawberries.
   c) be a gluten-free cake.
   d) exclude something traditional.

Diagram Variety

A variety of diagrams are used in Reading Part 2. In the following diagram, the information is presented in a more graphical manner than in the example on page 17. This highlights the need to closely read the wording of the email and connect it to specific information presented in the diagram. In order to complete the questions, you will have to continually refer back and forth between the email and the diagram.

Activity 2

Read the diagram and email and answer Questions 1–6. The thoughts of a high-level test taker have been provided in the Answer Key to show how she arrived at the correct answers. The last two questions in this practice for Reading Part 2 (Questions 7 and 8) deal specifically with tone and purpose, and they will appear later in this unit.

Reading Part 2: Reading to Apply a Diagram Time remaining: **9 minutes 0 seconds** **NEXT**

Welcome to the Ontario Driver's License Information Portal!

You need to be at least 16 years old to apply for a driver's license in Ontario. New drivers need to collect enough driving experience before they can complete the process. It takes most people about 20 months to get their full license. Here's how you can get a driver's license.

In order to determine the next steps in obtaining your license, please scroll down to the chart below.

Question #1
Have you ever had a driver's license? **NO** ➡ Please call 1-800-55-DRIVE to book your test. Fees will apply.

YES ⬇

Question #2
Is your driver's license from another province? **NO** ➡ Please visit your nearest Drive Ontario office.

YES ⬇

Question #3
Is your license still valid? **NO** ➡ Please visit your nearest Drive Ontario office.

YES ⬇

Please fill out "License Exchange form 55-2H." Fees will apply.

The Ontario driver's license is a blue plastic card that includes your name, address, date of birth, photo, and signature. The license has an expiry date of 5 years after the date of issue, with the exception of special circumstances. You have to renew your license before it expires; otherwise, additional steps may be required.

Questions? Please <u>click here</u> to contact an information agent or visit our <u>FAQ page</u>.

ⓘ Read the following email message about the diagram on the left. Complete the email by filling in the blanks. Select the best choice for each blank from the drop-down menu (▾).

From: sam@email.com
To: info@driveontario.on.ca
Subject: Questions

Hello,

I am new to Ontario, and I would like to get a driver's license. I 1. ⬚ ▾ but some details are unclear to me. I would like some help.

First of all, I am a driver from another province, but my license is no longer valid. According to the chart, I should 2. ⬚ ▾. If I am reading this correctly, there 3. ⬚ ▾. Also, my wife's license is still valid. It seems she should 4. ⬚ ▾ but we do not see it on this page. It is difficult for me to view this as an "information portal," since there 5. ⬚ ▾ I would recommend that this chart be updated soon, but in the meantime, please send us the required information.

Sincerely,

Sam Abbas

ⓘ Using the drop-down menu (▾), choose the best option.

6. What might be included with the agent's response? ⬚ ▾

7. Why did Sam write this email? ⬚ ▾

8. What is the tone of Sam's email? ⬚ ▾

Complete the email by filling in the blanks. Select the best choice for each blank from the options below.

1. a) went to your information desk
    b) read your brochure
    c) visited your website
    d) saw your bus advertisement

2. a) fill out a form
    b) visit an office
    c) call the hotline
    d) book a test

3. a) are no fees for this
    b) is only one office
    c) are a few forms to fill out
    d) is only one type of test

4. a) talk to a representative
    b) visit an office
    c) fill out a form
    d) book an appointment

5. a) are so many numbers for new drivers
    b) is a complete list of forms
    c) are such high fees for services
    d) is so much missing information

6. What might be included with the agent's response?
    a) a list of locations for driving tests
    b) the contact information for another agent
    c) the test appointment details
    d) a link to "Exchange Form 55-2H"

Identifying Purpose and Tone

In Activity 2, the questions required the test taker to match the wording of the email to specific information in the diagram. To answer this type of question, it is necessary to carefully read the details of the email and match them to the diagram. It is important to be able to identify paraphrases and synonyms here. However, in Reading Part 2, you may also be asked about purpose and tone. These types of questions rely less on your understanding of the diagram and more on being attuned to words that express intention and emotion in the text. Note that questions related to purpose and tone can appear in any part of the Reading Test.

Purpose

An author always writes with a purpose. It is your responsibility as the reader to analyze the information and determine what the purpose is. Many texts are written to **inform** readers of a concept or to **explain** new information (e.g., textbooks, newspapers, and diagrams). In some cases, authors present facts to **persuade** the reader (e.g., brochures, advertisements, and editorials). Other times, authors write for **entertainment** (e.g., magazines and novels).

On the CELPIP Test, it is important to understand what the purpose of the text is. To determine the purpose, you can look for the following:

AUDIENCE: If the text is an email, check to see who it is written to. If it is a diagram, article, or regular passage, try to determine who it is written for.

AUTHOR'S INTENTION: This may be expressed in a number of different ways. For example, it could appear in the subject line, or the opening or closing statements of an email. Sometimes, the author's purpose is evident in the body of the passage or email.

The author might be writing for various reasons, including:

- Asking for or giving opinions
- Expressing preferences
- Explaining and justifying
- Asking for advice or clarification

The purpose of the two example diagrams on pages 17 and 21 is mainly to inform the readers. The emails that follow each diagram have different purposes. The "Wedding Cake" email on page 19 is requesting help, whereas the "Driver's License" email on page 21 is asking for clarification.

Purpose questions normally ask you to identify the author's intention in writing the passage or email. The questions might look like this:

- Why did the author write this?
- What is the main concern of the author?
- What is the author intending to do?
- What is the author mainly concerned with?

Activity 3

Match the sample phrases on the left with the purposes on the right.

___ 1. I still can't find the information on the website. Could you be more specific . . .

a) explaining and justifying

___ 2. Would you advise me on the next step of the application process?

b) expressing preference

___ 3. Both seem like acceptable options, but I would rather have . . .

c) requesting

___ 4. The reason I had it postponed was mainly because . . .

d) asking for advice

___ 5. It would be great if you could send me the samples for . . .

e) asking for clarification

Activity 4

Now answer this question. This is a continuation of Activity 2 on page 21.

---

7. Why did Sam write this email?
   a) He would like to book his test.
   b) He has never driven before.
   c) He does not know the fees.
   d) He would like more information.

   Which information helped you identify the purpose of Sam's email?
   Select three options.

   ○ If I am reading this correctly,   ○ According to the chart,

   ○ . . . but some details are unclear to me.   ○ Subject: Questions

   ○ . . . please send us the required   ○ It is difficult for me to view this as an
     information.   "information portal," . . .

Tone

The author's tone reveals his attitude towards the subject he has written about. Tone is normally expressed through the words and details the author selects. In order to answer questions about tone, remember to look for emotionally charged language; this can provide clues to the writer's mood. To determine the author's tone, you must check for words that convey emotions and attitude, and also check for details that provide clues about the tone.

Activity 5

Writers can convey many different moods or tones through their wording. Here are some common examples of tone.

Positive	Negative
excited	disappointed
optimistic	sad
proud	morose
joking	angry
grateful	resentful
hopeful	critical
ecstatic	pessimistic

Identify the tone in the following sentences using the words in this chart. Underline words or phrases that provide clues about the tone of each sentence. The first one has been done for you.

1. Tomas, <u>I cannot believe</u> you <u>failed</u> that French test!
   Tone: <u>Disappointed</u>

2. Congratulations on passing your driving test, Prina!
   Tone: _____

3. I really appreciate all that you did for me.
   Tone: _____

4. This is the best day of my life! Jim has proposed and I'm so thrilled that we'll be getting married in 6 months!
   Tone: _____

5. Why would you say something so hurtful?
   Tone: _____

Activity 6

Now answer this question. This is a continuation of Activity 2 on page 21.

8. What is the tone of Sam's email?
   a) frustrated
   b) humorous
   c) worried
   d) excited

Which words and phrases gave you clues about the tone?
Select three options.

○ I would recommend this chart be updated soon . . .

○ It seems she should fill out a form . . .

○ I am new to Ontario . . .

○ I visited your website, but some information is unclear to me.

○ . . . but in the meantime . . .

○ . . . there is so much missing information.

Time Management

- **DIAGRAM**: Take about **1 minute** to **skim** the diagram and learn how it is organized.

- **EMAIL**: Take **1 more minute** to **skim** the email.

- **EMAIL ANSWERS**: Scan the diagram, and take **1 minute** for **each question**. Keep key points in mind as you skim.

- **FINAL QUESTIONS**: Leave at least **2 minutes** to complete the **three comprehension questions**, scanning both the diagram and the message for this last section.

Reading for Information

LEARNING FOCUS
- Recognizing components of a passage
- Identifying the topic
- Identifying main ideas
- Locating and listing supporting details
- Recognizing synonyms and paraphrased ideas
- Putting it all together

In Reading Part 3: Reading for Information, you are working with an article comprised of four paragraphs, followed by nine statements about the passage. For each statement, you must choose which paragraph, if any, contains that information. This part of the test assesses your ability to quickly identify the main idea of each paragraph, then find and understand the supporting details. You will also need to be able to recognize synonyms and paraphrases.

1

❶ Read the following passage.

2

A. Of the many job-search methods, informational interviews are one of the most effective ways of securing employment. These differ from job interviews in that the job seeker is not actively applying for a job, but merely gathering information and asking for advice in order to make career decisions. During job interviews, the employer asks the questions and makes a judgment about whether to hire the applicant or not. In an informational interview, the job seeker is interviewing someone employed in a particular field of work to learn about the job, the work environment, the company, and the qualifications, and to get the employee's opinion and advice.

B. As in any interview, it is imperative that the job seeker prepare for the informational interview. Since the job seeker will be visiting an employee within an organization, doing a little research about the organization is advisable. It's important to use the interview time efficiently by asking questions that aren't already answered on a company website. These questions, which should be prepared beforehand, can cover general information about the position, as well as details about the company and the field. Confirming the date, time, and location of the interview, as well as the name of the person being interviewed, will assist in making a good first impression.

C. Although less formal than a job interview, the informational interview requires presentable attire and somewhat formal behaviour. Some common features are the greeting, handshake, and eye contact. To avoid furiously taking notes, it's advisable to record the session, with permission from the person being interviewed. The job seeker should listen attentively to the answers in order to ask follow-up questions. This is the job seeker's chance to learn everything they need to know about the job. Leaving a positive impression is key, as the job seeker is making a connection at this company and may wish to contact them again in the future.

D. To close, the job seeker should thank the employee with a firm handshake and a smile, before taking their leave. The job seeker should definitely not ask for employment at this point, but asking permission to contact the employee if they have further questions is recommended. As a token of appreciation, sending a thank-you card is appropriate. Within a month after the interview, it's a nice gesture to send a short email with a comment on how the interview helped the job seeker. This also serves to solidify the connection.

E. Not given in any of the above paragraphs.

❶ Decide which paragraph, A to D, has the information given in each statement below. Select E if the information is not given in any of the paragraphs.

3

▾ - 1. The job seeker should prepare informed questions before the meeting.

▾ - 2. In an informational interview, the employee will request your resumé.

▾ - 3. There is no expectation of a job offer during an informational interview.

▾ - 4. In an informational interview, the roles are reversed compared to a job interview.

▾ - 5. Just as for a job interview, it is necessary to take care with your appearance.

▾ - 6. Following up after the interview is a worthwhile courtesy.

▾ - 7. In a job interview, the job seeker is expected to provide references.

4

- A
- B
- C
- D
- E

- 8. Making a personal contact can be beneficial when employment later.

- 9. The company sets up the informational interview seeker's request.

5

① **Main passage is informational text.**

② **Four paragraphs labelled A, B, C, D to match with answer choices.**

③ **There are nine questions presented as statements.**

④ **There are five answer choices: One for each paragraph, plus "E" when information in statement is not given in passage.**

⑤ **Answer "E" means information is not in paragraphs.**

Recognizing Components of a Passage

Understanding how information in a passage is structured will help you score well in this part of the test because you will be able to locate the necessary information quickly. There are three main components in a passage of text:

TOPIC:	This is the subject of the passage; it is usually introduced in the first paragraph.
MAIN IDEAS:	These directly support the topic. There is usually one main idea in each paragraph, but sometimes there could be two.
SUPPORTING DETAILS:	These give more information about the main idea of the paragraph by providing examples, facts, and descriptions; there are usually at least three supporting details in a paragraph.

A passage is like a house—it needs a good foundation (main ideas with supporting details) to hold up the roof (topic).

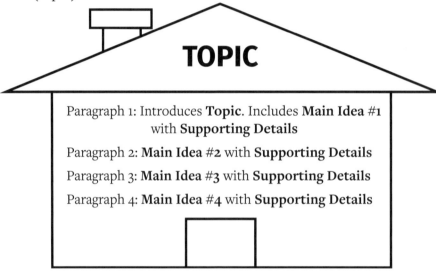

TOPIC

Paragraph 1: Introduces **Topic**. Includes **Main Idea #1** with **Supporting Details**

Paragraph 2: **Main Idea #2** with **Supporting Details**

Paragraph 3: **Main Idea #3** with **Supporting Details**

Paragraph 4: **Main Idea #4** with **Supporting Details**

Identifying the Topic

A quick look at the first sentence of each paragraph should help you identify the main topic of a reading passage. If you quickly skim the passage, you will see that each paragraph develops a main idea which supports that topic. In addition, the statements to the right of the reading refer to the same topic.

Activity 1

Look at the sample reading on page 27. Read the first sentence of each paragraph to identify the topic. If you are still unsure, skim the passage. Can you identify the topic in 30 seconds or less?

> The topic of this passage is:
> (select one only)
> - ○ job interviews.
> - ○ job search methods.
> - ○ informational interviews.
> - ○ job applications.

Identifying Main Ideas

A key skill in Reading for Information is being able to identify which paragraph contains the information you are looking for. Since you will not have time to read each paragraph carefully to determine the correct answer, you must learn to spot the main ideas in each paragraph. Once you know what each paragraph is about, it's much easier to narrow your options and find the information you are looking for.

> **Tip** One way to identify the main idea of each paragraph is to write down a few key words from each one. To help with this, you will be provided with notepaper when you take the official test.

Activity 2

Read the following paragraphs and select the statement that best expresses the main idea of each paragraph.

> A. Of the many job-search methods, informational interviews are one of the most effective ways of securing employment. These differ from job interviews in that the job seeker is not actively applying for a job, but merely gathering information and asking for advice in order to make career decisions. During job interviews, the employer asks the questions and makes a judgment about whether to hire the applicant or not. In an informational interview, the job seeker is interviewing someone employed in a particular field of work to learn about the job, the work environment, the company, and the qualifications, and to get the employee's opinion and advice.

1. a) Informational interviews are different from job interviews and can be very useful.
   b) In a job interview, the job seeker is expected to provide references.
   c) An informal interview is the only way to successfully obtain a new job.
   d) There are many types of job-search methods.

> B. As in any interview, it is imperative that the job seeker prepare for the informational interview. Since the job seeker will be visiting an employee within an organization, doing a little research about the organization is advisable. It's important to use the interview time efficiently by asking questions that aren't already answered on a company website. These questions, which should be prepared beforehand, can cover general information about the position, as well as details about the company and the field. Confirming the date, time, and location of the interview, as well as the name of the person being interviewed, will assist in making a good first impression.

2. a) The informational interview will determine whether an applicant is successful.

   (b) It is important to be ready for an informational interview.

   c) The company sets up the informational interview at the job seeker's request.

   d) An informational interview is a formal business event.

C. Although less formal than a job interview, the informational interview requires presentable attire and somewhat formal behaviour. Some common features are the greeting, handshake, and eye contact. To avoid furiously taking notes, it's advisable to record the session, with permission from the person being interviewed. The job seeker should listen attentively to the answers in order to ask follow-up questions. This is the job seeker's chance to learn everything they need to know about the job. Leaving a positive impression is key, as the job seeker is making a connection at this company and may wish to contact them again in the future.

3. a) In an informational interview, the employee will ask you many questions.

   b) The applicant should take meticulous notes throughout the interview.

   (c) Just as for a job interview, it is necessary to take care with your appearance and manner.

   d) Making a personal contact can be beneficial when seeking employment later.

D. To close, the job seeker should thank the employee with a firm handshake and a smile, before taking their leave. The job seeker should definitely not ask for employment at this point, but asking permission to contact the employee if they have further questions is recommended. As a token of appreciation, sending a thank-you card is appropriate. Within a month after the interview, it's a nice gesture to send a short email with a comment on how the interview helped the job seeker. This also serves to solidify the connection.
E. Not given in any of the above paragraphs.

4. a) The job seeker should be prepared to accept a job offer.

   (b) There are certain steps to follow both at the end of the interview and afterwards.

   c) The employee will set up a job interview after the informational interview.

   d) There is no expectation of a job offer during an informational interview.

Time Management
- Main passage: 1 minute, maximum
- 9 questions: 1 minute/question, maximum

Locating and Listing Supporting Details

After you have taken about a minute to identify the main ideas in each of the paragraphs in Reading Part 3, look at the nine statements on the right. Once you have read over one of the statements, try to identify which paragraph likely contains the matching information. Next, you will have to locate supporting details in that paragraph that may correspond to the information in the statement. If the supporting details do not match the statement, you will need to continue checking paragraphs until you can find a match, or determine that the information in the statement is not contained in the passage.

The ability to quickly locate supporting details will help you determine where, if anywhere, the information in each statement is located in the passage. The following activity will help you develop this useful skill.

Activity 3

Read Paragraph A of the passage on page 27 again. In Activity 2, Question 1, you learned that the main idea for this paragraph is that informational interviews can be very useful during a job search. Now select all the supporting details that helped you identify the topic.

> Select all the answers that apply.
> - ○ Employers conduct job interviews.
> - ◉ Informational interviews allow people to learn about a particular field.
> - ○ There are many types of interviews for jobs.
> - ◉ The purpose of informational interviews is to gather information.
> - ○ Practicing interview skills is important before attending a job interview.
> - ◉ Employees share their views of the job, work environment, company, and qualifications with people interested in the field.

Activity 4

Decide which paragraph, A to D, has the information given in each statement below. Select E if the information is not given in any of the paragraphs. The first two have been done for you. Explanations have been provided in the Answer Key.

> __B__ 1. The job seeker should prepare informed questions before the meeting.
>
> __E__ 2. In an informational interview, the employee will request your resumé.
>
> __D__ 3. There is no expectation of a job offer during an informational interview.
>
> __A__ 4. In an informational interview, the roles are reversed compared to a job interview.
>
> __C__ 5. Just as for a job interview, it is necessary to take care with your appearance.
>
> __E__ 6. Following up after the interview is a worthwhile courtesy. D
>
> __E__ 7. In a job interview, the job seeker is expected to provide references.
>
> __D__ 8. Making a personal contact can be beneficial when seeking employment later. C
>
> __E__ 9. The company sets up the informational interview at the job seeker's request.

Recognizing Synonyms and Paraphrased Ideas

In Reading for Information, most of the nine statements will contain paraphrased information from the passage. You saw this in Activity 4. The statement will have the same meaning as a section of the text, but it may be expressed using different words. The ability to recognize an idea written in a different way, as well as identifying synonyms for key words, will help you to answer the questions in Reading for Information.

Activity 5A

In Reading for Information, it is important to be able to identify synonyms and paraphrases so that you can connect a statement to information in the passage. Complete the chart below by matching the words or phrases with the same meaning. Write the letter next to the number.

✗ k	1. unusual	a) creature	
g	2. financial backing	b) unique	
l	3. justifiably	c) filter	
✗ i	4. organism	d) in good condition	
ρ e	5. modern day k	e) in total	
✓ c	6. purify	f) underwater	
✓ h	7. site	g) funding	
ρ a	8. well-preserved d	h) location	
✗ d	9. altogether e	i) groups	
✓ b	10. exceptional	j) odd	
✓ F	11. submerged	k) contemporary	
ρ j	12. clusters i	l) rightly	

Activity 5B ✓

Now match the information on the left with the paraphrased statement on the right. Write the letter next to the appropriate number. The paraphrased statements contain some of the synonyms from the activity above.

	INFORMATION FROM PASSAGE	PARAPHRASED STATEMENT
b	1. Researchers require financial backing to search for well-preserved fossils.	a) Contemporary ocean dwellers bear no resemblance to the odd organisms that lived millions of years ago.
e	2. It is believed that clusters of these ancient creatures gathered on the ocean floor.	b) Funding is required if scientists are to discover fossils in good condition.
a	3. These unusual prehistoric creatures were entirely different from modern-day fish.	c) Researchers found the remains at an underwater site.
c	4. The fossils were found at a site submerged deep in the ocean.	d) Researchers were rightly surprised when they found proof of unique organisms like these.
d	5. Scientists were justifiably amazed to discover these exceptional creatures.	e) Researchers feel that groups of these prehistoric organisms collected at the bottom of the sea.

Putting It All Together

Using all the skills you have learned in this unit, see how quickly you can identify the topic, main ideas, and supporting details in this new passage. Some of the wording and ideas have already been introduced in Activities 5A and 5B.

Activity 6

Read the following passage from *Reading for Information*. Then fill in the missing information in the chart on the next page. Some of the notes have been completed to help you get started.

A. In early 2012, a strange fossilized creature was discovered in the Burgess Shale of the Canadian Rockies. Lorna O'Brien, then a doctoral candidate in the Department of Ecology and Evolutionary Biology at the University of Toronto, and her supervisor, Jean-Bernard Caron, curator of invertebrate paleontology at the Royal Ontario Museum, reported the find. Their research was partially funded by the University of Toronto and Canada's Natural Sciences and Engineering Research Council (NSERC) through a fellowship and a grant, respectively.

B. The Burgess Shale, a site protected by UNESCO and managed by Parks Canada, is justifiably famous since it contains exceptionally well-preserved fossil evidence of some of the earliest complex animals, mostly soft-bodied, that lived in the oceans of our planet. The region where the creature was first discovered is located in Yoho National Park, British Columbia, high on Mount Stephen and overlooking the town of Field. The rock in which the fossil was found is 500 million years old, which means the creature lived 500 million years ago. Since the rock was submerged at that time, it would have been an ocean-dwelling creature.

C. The fossilized remains indicate that the creature, Siphusauctum gregarium, was the length of a dinner knife, about 20 cm. It had a tulip-shaped body with a stem ending in a small disc. O'Brien and Caron hypothesize that this disc anchored it to the ocean floor. It also had a cup-like top. Since the researchers have discovered single slabs of rock containing the remains of more than 65 Siphusauctum gregarium individuals, they infer that the creatures lived in garden-like clusters on the sea floor. Altogether, they have discovered more than a thousand individual organisms in the area, which has been nicknamed "the tulip beds."

D. Siphusauctum gregarium has not been the only strange creature discovered in the Burgess Shale. In fact, that part of the Rockies has a reputation for weird discoveries. However, unlike Siphusauctum gregarium, most of the odd creatures are primitive versions of contemporary animals. This does not appear to be true of Siphusauctum gregarium.

What is unique about this creature is its feeding system, as it is thought to have fed by filtering particles from water that it pumped through small holes in its cup-like top. The discovery of Siphusauctum gregarium is important, therefore, in part because it indicates that there was more diversity among animals at the time than was previously thought.

E. Not given in any of the above paragraphs.

Topic: New fossil discovery
OR *Siphusauctum gregarium*

Paragraph A

Main Idea: The people who made the discovery

- 2012

- Fossil discovered

- Canadian Rockies

- Royal Ontario Museum

- University of Toronto

Paragraph B

Main Idea: The Burgess Shale is protected by UNESCO

- Has fossil remains of earliest animals

- first discover Yoho National Park

- Soft bodies

- 500 million years old

- Creature lives 500 millions years

Paragraph C

Main Idea: About *Siphusauctum gregarium*

- About 20 cm long

- tulip-shaped body ✓

- Stem ending in a small disc

- live in garden like clusters

- nick named Tulip beds

Paragraph D

Main Idea: Strange discoveries

-

-

-

-

Test Practice

Use the skills you have learned in this unit to complete these test questions for the fossil passage on page 33. Decide which paragraph, A to D, has the information given in each statement below. Select E if the information is not given in any of the paragraphs.

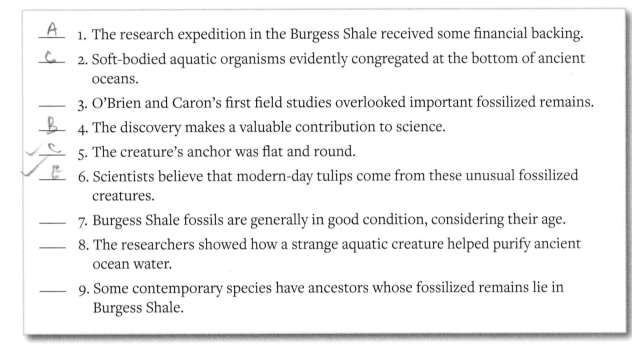

_A_   1. The research expedition in the Burgess Shale received some financial backing.

_C_   2. Soft-bodied aquatic organisms evidently congregated at the bottom of ancient oceans.

_____   3. O'Brien and Caron's first field studies overlooked important fossilized remains.

_B_   4. The discovery makes a valuable contribution to science.

_C_   5. The creature's anchor was flat and round.

_E_   6. Scientists believe that modern-day tulips come from these unusual fossilized creatures.

_____   7. Burgess Shale fossils are generally in good condition, considering their age.

_____   8. The researchers showed how a strange aquatic creature helped purify ancient ocean water.

_____   9. Some contemporary species have ancestors whose fossilized remains lie in Burgess Shale.

Reading for Viewpoints

LEARNING FOCUS	• Differentiating between facts and opinions
	• Identifying viewpoints
	• Identifying opinions
	• Understanding new words

Reading Part 4: Reading for Viewpoints features an online article about a topical issue and includes a short reader's comment. It tests your ability to integrate information from different parts of the passage, identify opinions, differentiate between opinions and facts, and make inferences. You will be reading about different experts' opinions on the same topic, which could relate to business, economics, social policy, education, science, technology, or other topics. The vocabulary and sentence structure in this last part of the Reading Test can be challenging.

Reading Part 4: Reading for Viewpoints

Time remaining: 13 minutes 0 seconds **NEXT**

ℹ Read the following article from a website.

Advances in sanitation, medical technology, and agricultural productivity have allowed population growth to reach unprecedented peaks since the 1950s. According to a study by demographist Farzad Farzi, the world population, which stood at approximately 3 billion in 1959, is expected to reach 7.7 billion in 2020, before peaking at between 9 to 11 billion people in 2050. "Such rapid population expansion is raising fears that the number of humans could exceed the carrying capacity of the planet, leading to a rapid depletion of non-renewable resources and an escalation in the amount of war, famine, and environmental degradation."

"World population is already above sustainable levels. Overpopulation is having a visible impact on water quality, air pollution, deforestation, biodiversity, desertification, and much more," stated Sujoy Gupta, a researcher with the Northern Nature Foundation. "We have to implement population control methods such as family planning and tax measures to limit population growth before it becomes a catastrophe," he claimed.

Not everyone is alarmed by global overpopulation, however. Kelly Wong, a demography professor at Athabasca University, argues that population growth is leveling off of its own accord. "As people move to the city, children come to be seen as an economic burden that hinders material success, and the birth rate, consequently, tends to fall off naturally." She also claims that issues of war, famine, and environmental degradation are not brought about by overpopulation, but, rather, are facts of life that have been with us from time immemorial.

Others are even more drastic in their attitude towards overpopulation. "I don't worry about overpopulation anymore," indicated Lucinda Maxwell, an environmental activist based in Halifax. "Population growth is slowing, but per capita consumption has skyrocketed. Most of the extra consumption is happening in rich countries that have long since stopped seeing substantial population growth. It's not enough to control population growth. Unless we change our consumption habits, we'll eventually witness resource shortages and a degradation of living conditions across the planet. Consumption and inequality are really the elephants in the room when we are talking about overpopulation."

ℹ Using the drop-down menu (▾), choose the best option according to the information given on the website.

1. Which word best describes Farzad Farzi's attitude toward population growth? [▾]
   - ○ a) skeptical.
   - ○ b) dismal.
   - ○ c) surprised.
   - ○ d) indifferent.
2. What would Sujoy [...] encourage? [▾]
3. What does Kelly W[...] [▾]
4. What does Lucinda Maxwell likely believe? [▾]
5. The most appropriate title for this article is [▾]

ℹ The following is a comment by a visitor to the website page. Complete the comment by choosing the best option to fill in each blank.

Working for the Canadian government in the developing world, I would tend to agree with Ms. Maxwell when she argues that 6. [▾] . As both Maxwell and Wong indicate, population growth has been slowing down, and urbanization in developing countries means that future population growth will likely 7. [▾] . The statistics provided by Farzi on future population growth, therefore, 8. [▾] .

What should be of greater concern than population, 9. [▾] , is the fact that consumption is rising and mainly occurs in the developed world. By focusing on overpopulation as the root cause of social and environmental ills, 10. [▾] might unintentionally be blaming the poor for a problem that has more to do with the rich nations of the world.

① Main passage is website posting.

② Keep track of your time with countdown timer.

③ There are ten questions in total.

④ First five questions refer to main passage.

⑤ There are five text-completion questions for comment about website.

37

Differentiating Between Facts and Opinions

In Reading for Viewpoints, you will need to identify key facts, understand the experts' opinions, and demonstrate that you can recognize the difference between facts and opinions. One useful strategy is to watch out for key indicator words that introduce a statement that is either a fact or opinion. In the following exercise, try to identify indicator words as well as the overall meaning of the sentence to help you decide if each statement expresses a fact or an opinion.

Activity 1

Read each statement and circle "fact" or "opinion." Explanations are provided in the Answer Key.

1. Farzad Farzi reported that the world population is expected to reach 7.7 billion in 2020. ⟨FACT⟩ or OPINION

2. Lucinda Maxwell has looked at the numbers to verify that population growth is now finally slowing down. FACT or OPINION

3. The mayor, who does not own a car, stated that the city will soon be introducing more dedicated bike lanes. FACT or OPINION

4. Many politicians assert that the government must put better measures in place to deal with problems related to population growth, especially in developing countries. FACT or OPINION

5. A recently published article demonstrated that in the past few years the need for separated bike lanes has increased. ⟨FACT⟩ or OPINION

6. Experts disclosed that improvements in medicine, farming, and hygiene have contributed to the population boom. ⟨FACT⟩ or OPINION

7. The mayor's critics have argued that his bike-friendly approach will cause more traffic congestion. FACT or ⟨OPINION⟩

8. Lucinda Maxwell realized that people are spending significantly more in countries where there has been no recent increase in population. FACT or OPINION

9. Some environmentalists believe that our spending habits are just as problematic as population growth. FACT or OPINION

10. Gregor Robertson insisted that the city will see the profoundly positive impact of bike lanes in the future. FACT or ⟨OPINION⟩

11. Kelly Wong contends that population growth is actually slowing down. FACT or OPINION

12. The latest numbers indicate that by spring 2017, Vancouver will be among Lyon, Paris, Montreal, and other cities that have a bike system for the public. ⟨FACT⟩ or OPINION

Activity 2

Read the paragraph below and answer the questions. Watch for indicator words used to introduce a fact or an opinion to help you complete this activity. Explanations have been provided in the Answer Key.

> This article demonstrates that there is a serious and ongoing disagreement in Vancouver between bicycle riders and car owners. Mayor Gregor Robertson, who does not own a car, stated that the city will be introducing more dedicated bike lanes in the coming year as well as raising the cost of residential parking permits by 750%, from $80 to $600 per year. Car owners contend that this steep increase is unacceptable and unaffordable. Bicycle riders have argued that there are thousands of available parking spaces in underground parking lots that car owners could rent at reasonable rates. The city government, however, insists that eliminating affordable parking zones will benefit the public by forcing people to access busy areas by public transit or bicycle. Both government experts and cycling enthusiasts believe that there is no solution in sight yet for this disagreement.

1. What does Mayor Gregor Robertson believe? *opinion*
    a) More parking in busy city areas will result in more business.
    b) Car owners should be able to purchase inexpensive indoor parking spaces.
    c) Taking away inexpensive parking spaces is good for the public.

2. What do car owners assert? *opinion*
    a) Drivers should have access to affordable parking.
    b) Cyclists should pay to park underground.
    c) There are enough affordable parking zones in the city.

3. What is it that cyclists feel? *opinion*
    a) Parking availability for cars in the downtown core is not a serious problem.
    b) Dedicated bike lanes will reduce traffic congestion.
    c) There is no obvious resolution for this problem.

4. *Fact*
    What did Mayor Gregor Robertson confirm about the cost of parking permits?
    a) They will rise significantly for downtown residents.
    b) They will fall slightly for downtown residents.
    c) They will remain the same.

Identifying Viewpoints

In Reading for Viewpoints, you may be asked to express the viewpoint of the writer by selecting the best title or choosing the statement that accurately summarizes the main idea of the article. You may also be asked to identify one individual's opinion or viewpoint about a certain aspect of the topic.

There may be one test question that asks you to identify the main idea of a passage. This question could be worded in several different ways. Here are some common examples:

- Based on the article . . .
- According to the article . . .
- The article's main point is . . .
- The most appropriate title is . . .

To identify the main idea of a passage, you need to understand the main idea in each paragraph and how they all fit together to express an attitude or opinion.

Activity 3 ✗

Look at the article on page 37 and answer the question below. Check your answer in the Answer Key.

> The most appropriate title for this article is
> a) Population Growth: Should We Be Alarmed?
> b) Global Overpopulation: What Are the Causes?
> c) Overpopulation Triggers Natural Disasters
> d) Curbing Today's Global Overpopulation

The article is shown below with key information highlighted. The small blue boxes provide explanations about how the main idea in each paragraph helps us understand the main viewpoint presented in the article, and one key word is given at the end of each box to convey the overall attitude of the paragraph.

Advances in sanitation, medical technology, and agricultural productivity have allowed population growth to reach **unprecedented peaks** since the 1950s. According to a study by demographist Farzad Farzi, the world population, which stood at approximately 3 billion in 1959, is expected to reach 7.7 billion in 2020, before peaking at between 9 to 11 billion people in 2050. "Such rapid population expansion is **raising fears** that the number of humans could exceed the carrying capacity of the planet, leading to a rapid depletion of non-renewable resources and an escalation in the amount of war, famine, and environmental degradation."

des pics sans précédent
se tenir a
de premier plan
escalade

> This paragraph expresses concerns about:
> - Highest world population ever
> - Too many people on the planet
> - Not enough resources
> **FEAR!**

au-dessus des niveaux convenables

"World population is already **above sustainable levels.** Overpopulation is having a visible impact on water quality, air pollution, deforestation, biodiversity, desertification, and much more," stated Sujoy Gupta, a researcher with the Northern Nature Foundation. "We have to implement population control methods such as family planning and tax measures to limit population growth **before it becomes a catastrophe**," he claimed.

> All these people are affecting our water, air, wildlife, land, etc.
> **CATASTROPHE!**

> This paragraph confirms that some people—but not all—find overpopulation alarming. Note the use of the word **ALARM**, which is part of the correct answer choice.

Not everyone is alarmed by global overpopulation, however. Kelly Wong, a demography professor at Athabasca University, argues that population growth is levelling off of its own accord. "As people move to the city, children come to be seen as an economic burden that hinders material success, and the birth rate, consequently, tends to fall off naturally." She also claims that issues of war, famine, and environmental degradation are not brought about by overpopulation, but, rather, are facts of life that have been with us from time immemorial.

Others are even more drastic in their attitude towards overpopulation. "I don't worry about overpopulation anymore," indicated Lucinda Maxwell, an environmental activist based in Halifax. "Population growth is slowing, but per capita consumption has skyrocketed. Most of the extra consumption is happening in rich countries that have long since stopped seeing substantial population growth. It's not enough to control population growth. Unless we change our consumption habits, we'll eventually witness **resource shortages** and a **degradation of living conditions** across the planet. Consumption and inequality are really the elephants in the room when we are talking about overpopulation."

> The highlighted terms in this paragraph add strength to the main idea of this passage. Words like "drastic," "shortages," and "degradation" reinforce the negative feelings associated with **OVERPOPULATION**.

Identifying Opinions

Test questions often ask you to identify one expert's opinion, confirm which two experts have the same opinion, or decide which expert disagrees with another expert. The questions may use words such as "attitude," "believe/belief," or "opinion." Here are several examples of how these questions could be phrased:

- We can tell that Mr. X's opinion is . . .
- As Mr. Z indicates . . .
- John asserts that . . .
- Mrs. X and Mr. Y likely believe that . . .
- Unlike Herbert, Mikako argues that . . .

Activity 4

Look back at the article beginning on page 40 to identify each required opinion and choose the best answer. The information provided in the blue boxes will help, and detailed explanations are provided in the Answer Key.

1. Which word best describes Farzad Farzi's attitude toward population growth?
   a) skeptical
   b) dismal   *lugubre*
   c) surprised
   d) indifferent

2. What would Sujoy Gupta likely encourage?
   a) expanding urban development to the suburbs
   b) greater tax breaks for large families
   c) government restrictions on household size   *la teuille dos ménage*
   d) limiting relief funds for natural disasters

3. What does Kelly Wong assert?
   a) population growth damages the economy
   b) people are abandoning urban centres
   c) changing values will offset population growth
   d) rising populations give rise to war and famine

4. What does Lucinda Maxwell likely believe?
   a) the way goods are consumed worldwide is imbalanced
   b) population growth is mainly an issue in wealthy nations
   c) the environmental effects of overpopulation are minor
   d) consumption rates in underdeveloped countries are too high

Activity 5

Here is the Reader's Comment for the article you've already seen. Read the comment and complete the test questions.

The following is a comment by a visitor to the website page.

Working for the Canadian government in the developing world, I would tend to **agree** with **Ms. Maxwell** when she argues that 6. ˅ . As both Maxwell and Wong indicate, population growth has been slowing down, and urbanization in developing countries means that **future population growth will likely 7.** ˅ . The statistics provided by **Farzi** on future population growth, **in fact,** 8. ˅ .

> "Agree" is a clear indicator of whose opinion this writer favours. Look for words like this in your readings; they will help guide your answers.

> The writer mentions both Maxwell and Wong in this sentence. What is something they both agree on, with regards to future population growth?

> From Activity 4, you already know that Farzi has a very pessimistic view, whereas Maxwell and Wong are less concerned. "In fact" indicates a comparison of opinions here.

What should be of greater concern than population, 9. ▾ , is the fact that consumption is rising and occurs mainly in the developed world. By focusing on overpopulation as the root cause of social and environmental ills, 10. ▾ might unintentionally be blaming the poor for a problem that has more to do with the rich nations of the world.

> The statement "consumption is rising and occurs mainly..." is the main idea here. Which of the options in Question 9 relates to this statement?

> Which individual holds the opinion that overpopulation is the "root cause of social and environmental ills?"

---

6. **(a)** population rates are not to blame for environmental woes *malhaurs*
   b) the people in developed countries are to blame
   c) Farzi's statistics on population growth are inaccurate
   d) the population in developing regions needs to be controlled

7. a) need to be stimulated
   b) fall in the study's predicted range
   (c) continue its downward trend
   d) increase at a faster rate

8. **(a)** might not be very accurate (*précis*)
   b) could be p̲r̲omising *prometteur*
   c) are quite accurate
   d) are actually positive

9. **(a)** as mentioned at the end of the article
   b) in line with the quoted study's forecast
   c) as the demography professor predicts
   d) contrary to the environmentalist's claims

10. a) the author
    (b) Wong
    c) Gupta ✓
    d) Maxwell

Time Management

- **WEBSITE ARTICLE:** Take up to **2 minutes** to **skim** this for general understanding.
- **FIVE QUESTIONS:** Take about **1 minute** for **each question**. This includes looking at the answer choices.
- **READER'S COMMENT:** Take **1 minute** to **skim** the comment and relate it to the article. This leaves you with **1 minute** for **each question** in the comment.

Watch the time carefully for this final Reading part! Focus only on the phrases and sentences that will help you find the answers you need.

Understanding New Words

The Reading Test gets more difficult as you move from Part 1 to Part 4. While the vocabulary may be fairly easy to understand at the beginning of the test, higher-level words and expressions are used more frequently towards the end. Since you can't bring a dictionary into the test room, it is important to develop a strategy for dealing with unknown words. This is especially important for Reading for Viewpoints.

It's not necessary to understand every word to perform well in this part of the test. When you come across a word that you don't know, you will have to decide whether it is important or not. Words that appear only once within a text are not as important to understand as those that are used several times. It is often possible to guess the meaning of a word by looking at the words and sentences around it for clues. Learn to stay calm and focused by searching for clues to help you understand these new words and phrases from the context of the sentence or paragraph. The next activity will help you understand how to find these clues.

Activity 6

The blanks in this passage all represent the same word. Read through the passage and look for clues to help you discover what the missing word is.

The history of _____ and humans dates back thousands of years. Many cultures have placed great importance on _____ since it was first written about in China in 2700 BC. This substance has been the subject of many stories; it has been part of important religious rituals; it has started wars; and it has even been used as currency in some cultures. The Bible has more than 30 references to this grainy element.

Many people may not be aware that _____ played a key role in world history. More than 2,000 years ago, China turned a tax on _____ into a major revenue source. Greece traded slaves for this valuable substance, and Roman soldiers received payment in the form of _____.

_____ has also had a major effect on humanity through food consumption, food preservation, and industrial uses. This white granular substance is essential to people, animals, and even some plants. Most people don't realize that this seasoning found on most dining tables has played such a vital role in human history, religion, economics, warfare—and health!

---

1. What is the missing word?

   _____ Salt _____

2. Select the clues that helped you guess the missing word:
   - ☒ This substance has been the subject of many stories. ✗
   - ☒ it has even been used as currency *devise* ✗
   - ☒ grainy element *élément granuleux*
   - ○ major revenue source
   - ☒ food consumption, food preservation ✓
   - ☒ white granular substance ✓
   - ○ essential to people
   - ☒ this seasoning found on most dining tables ✓

There should have been enough clues in this passage, especially in the third paragraph, to help you guess the unknown word (check the Answer Key if you're not sure). You can apply this same method to understand unfamiliar words in the CELPIP-General Reading Test. Let's now look at part of a new passage from Reading for Viewpoints. See if you can apply what you've learned to understand new words in this reading without using a dictionary.

Activity 7

Guess the meaning of the underlined word or phrase in each item below by looking for clues in the surrounding sentence(s).

> Vocal fry ("creaky voice") is an extremely low-pitched growl in the voice. Once heard mainly in males, "fry" has become a widespread <u>trait</u> of young women's voices, especially at the ends of statements or sentences, when the voice suddenly drops into the bass register. *→ caracter*
>
> Career coach Pamela Lindor describes vocal fry as a deliberate and widely copied affectation of young female American celebrities. Lindor grants that fry is perceived by many young people as a sign of "cool" urban upward mobility, but she <u>warns</u> that it carries a different meaning in the corporate workplace. <u>Lindor</u> cites a recent study by researcher Caroline Kaminski which concludes that women with vocal fry are perceived as less competent and less trustworthy. "Fry signals you're bored, world-weary, <u>enervated</u> *énervé* —not the image you want in the boardroom or at the podium," Lindor confidently <u>opines</u>. "You want to sound engaged, energized, committed to your intentions." Lindor urges women to reclaim their power by shunning vocal fry.
>
> Harvard University sociolinguist Shannon Thomas says Lindor is citing <u>flawed research</u>. "The speakers in the Kaminski study were feigning vocal fry. Listeners were likely reacting negatively to the artifice, not the fry," says Thomas, who regards the fry trend as a broad-based language shift. "Young women are at the forefront of this evolutionary change,

appropriating the bass register formerly the exclusive domain of males. The late great Douglas Hawkins and many other male news broadcasters were <u>renowned</u> for their fry. Why should a bass pitch be praised in men but scorned in women? Maybe the attack on fry is just a way of trying to silence female voices."

Speech pathologist Annabelle Wong has another take. "We hear some degree of fry in all speech, and it's common in popular singing. But habitual fry in either gender may be a sign of vocal cord <u>misuse</u> or damage. Yes, listeners may respond negatively, but not necessarily because they assume you're irresponsible. It's because they unconsciously perceive the reduced vocal energy as a subtle sign of <u>suboptimal</u> vocal health."

1. "Trait" means
   a) characteristic
   b) fear
   c) benefit

2. "Enervated" means
   a) aggravated
   b) exhausted
   c) excited

3. "Opines" means
   a) disagrees
   b) suggests
   c) infers

4. "Renowned" means
   a) paid
   b) hated
   c) famous

5. "Suboptimal" means
   a) superior
   b) inferior
   c) growing

Test Practice

Use everything you've learned and practiced in this unit to complete the Reading for Viewpoints questions below. Practice your time management skills by answering all the questions within 13 minutes.

1. The article's main point is that vocal fry
   a) could either hinder or boost a woman's career.
   b) may be a subtle symptom of a health problem.
   c) should be accepted in both men and women.
   d) is an emerging trait of debatable significance.

2. Who most clearly agrees with Kaminski?
   a) Hawkins
   b) Lindor
   c) Thomas
   d) Wong

3. When Lindor expresses her opinion, we can tell that she feels
   a) fashionable.
   b) self-assured.
   c) insecure.
   d) unpopular.

4. What does Thomas think about the researcher's conclusions?
   a) They are absurd.
   b) They are exaggerated.
   c) They are misguided.
   d) They are vague.

5. For whom would this article be of most relevance?
   a) People who follow historical figures in US news broadcasting
   b) People who follow news about American popular media stars
   c) People who follow research on treating vocal cord injuries
   d) People who follow social trends related to oral language use

Complete the comment by choosing the one best option to fill in each blank.

I recently re-entered the corporate workplace after working at home for 15 years.
6.   ▾ I'm uniquely qualified to confirm that women's voices have indeed become "fried." I'll side with the 7.   ▾ in contending that vocal fry makes people sound too lazy and lackadaisical to finish their statements. By the same token, I part ways with Shannon Thomas, who is obviously 8.   ▾ vocal fry. Moreover, 9.   ▾ , I think Douglas Hawkins would agree with Lindor that female vocal fry is not professionally appropriate.

I hear frequent, deliberate vocal fry among healthy female 20-somethings, but my older female colleagues "fry" only when they're tired or sick—and they apologize. Clearly, vocal fry is not just a health issue and a gender issue but also—as Thomas implies—10   ▾ .

6. a) Unless I return,
   b) More specifically,
   c) In spite of that,
   d) For that reason,

7. a) career coach
   b) sociolinguistic expert
   c) news broadcaster
   d) speech pathologist

8. a) a feminist adversary of
   b) a pseudo expert on
   c) an avid practitioner of
   d) an academic defender

9. a) having read his scholarly research
   b) if he were still here among us
   c) though few have heard of him
   d) when I hear him speak in public

10. a) an intractable habit
    b) an evolutionary advantage
    c) a journalistic debate
    d) a generational difference

LEARNING FOCUS
- Format of the Writing Test
- Scoring
- Improving your writing

The Writing Test measures your ability to communicate in ordinary day-to-day situations. It is made up of two tasks: writing an email and responding to survey questions. In Task 1, you may be asked, for example, to write an email complaining about a restaurant experience or requesting time off from your job. In Task 2, you will be asked to select one of two options and explain your preference. Examples of survey topics include childcare in the workplace or proposed changes to a school lunch program.

In this unit, you will become familiar with the overall format of the Writing Test. You will also learn about the four categories of the performance standards used by CELPIP Raters to assess your writing.

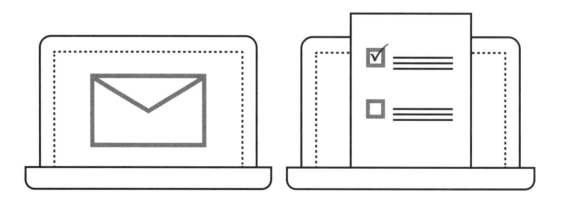

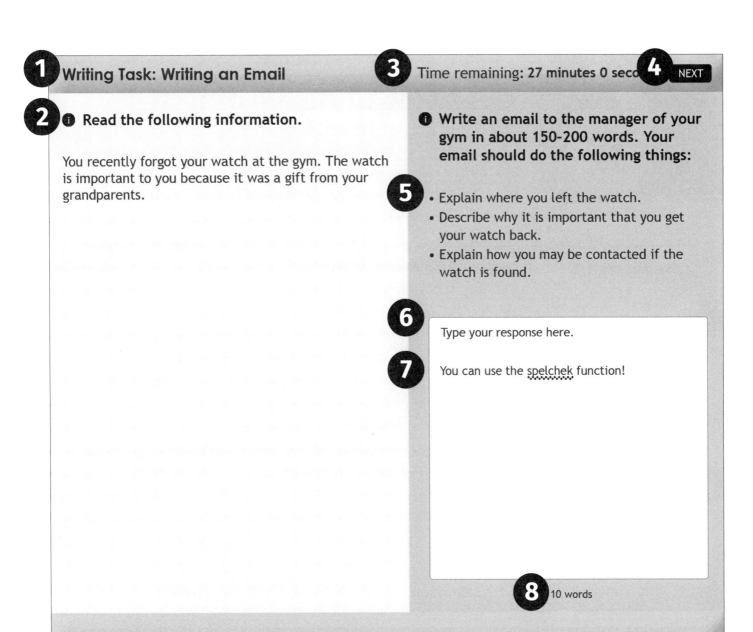

Writing Task: Writing an Email

Time remaining: 27 minutes 0 sec NEXT

ⓘ **Read the following information.**

You recently forgot your watch at the gym. The watch is important to you because it was a gift from your grandparents.

ⓘ **Write an email to the manager of your gym in about 150-200 words. Your email should do the following things:**

- Explain where you left the watch.
- Describe why it is important that you get your watch back.
- Explain how you may be contacted if the watch is found.

Type your response here.

You can use the spelchek function!

10 words

① Title reminds you where you are in test.

② Important background information is always on left.

③ Countdown timer shows how much time you have left for this page. When timer reaches zero, test will move to next part.

④ Use NEXT button to move to next part before timer reaches zero. You cannot move back.

⑤ You will always be asked to do three or four things, or choose between two options.

⑥ This is the typing area.

⑦ Basic editing tools make it easier to organize content, rework phrases and sentences, and correct mistakes. There are six editing functions: spell check, cut, paste, delete, undo, and redo.

⑧ The computer counts your words.

Format of the Writing Test

Each writing screen has the same basic format.

WRITING TASK	DESCRIPTION	WORD COUNT
Writing an Email	• Write an email about a common matter.	150–200 words
Responding to Survey Questions	• Respond to a survey question regarding workplace or community issues, and give reasons for your choice.	150–200 words
TOTAL TIME	**About 1 hour**	

Tip
- Read **all** instructions to the right of this "instructions" symbol 🛈 very carefully.
- Each task is the same length.
- These are not essays; they are writing tasks related to your home or work life.
- Once you move to Task 2, you cannot return to Task 1.
- You cannot add unused time from Task 1 to Task 2.

Scoring

Each task is worth 50% of your final Writing score. CELPIP Raters assess your writing in these four categories:

Content/Coherence:	Quality of ideas and how well they flow together
Vocabulary:	Selection and use of vocabulary, phrases, and idioms
Readability:	Understandability and fluency in your writing
Task Fulfillment:	Completion of all task requirements

The list below identifies the key features of each of these four categories that contribute to a high-scoring response.

Content/Coherence

- Ideas are strong and relevant.
- Ideas are clear, well organized, and easy to follow.
- Ideas have been combined effectively, with supporting details, to form a meaningful and coherent response.

Vocabulary

- Vocabulary demonstrates a range of suitable words and phrases.
- Words and phrases have been combined effectively to express precise meaning.
- Selected words and phrases support easy understanding.

Readability

- Response demonstrates good control of spelling, punctuation, and grammar.
- Response includes a variety of sentence types.
- Response includes appropriate paragraphing, formatting, and use of connectors and transitions.

Task Fulfillment

- Response addresses all parts of the task and follows the given instructions.
- Tone is appropriate for the situation.
- Overall purpose of the task has been achieved within the given word count.

Improving Your Writing

In preparing for the Writing Test, there are various ways to improve your skills. Practice writing as often as you can, whether it's in the form of emails to friends, family, or co-workers; or even a diary or blog. In addition, you may wish to keep a daily journal of new English words and phrases that you've learned. Review these terms frequently, and try to use them in your writing whenever you can; this will help increase your range of vocabulary.

LEARNING FOCUS

- Formatting your message
- Relating tone, task, and register
- Creating an outline
- Staying on topic
- Demonstrating range of vocabulary
- Using time sequencers and conjunctions
- Correcting your errors

In Writing Task 1: Writing an Email, you are given a short description of a situation together with specific instructions in bullet point format. Look at the infographic on the next page to learn more about these two parts of the task. Before you start planning and writing, use the information in the description and instructions to decide on the purpose, approach, content, and tone of your message.

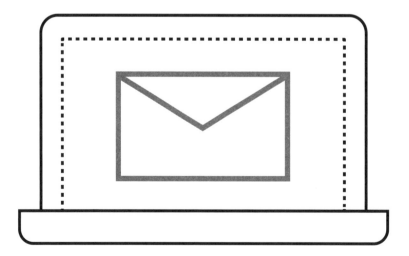

3 Time remaining: 27 minutes 0 se...   **4** NEXT

1 ℹ **Read the following information.**

2 You live in an apartment building that has a no-dogs policy. Renters are only allowed to have cats. You moved into the building a few months ago, and you keep hearing a dog barking in the next-door apartment, especially at night.

ℹ **Write an email to your building manager in about 150-200 words. Your email should do the following things:**

5 • Explain what you are experiencing.
• Complain about the dogs in the building.
• Suggest how the problem should be solved.

Type your response here.

4 words

① This section will describe the situation you will be writing about.

② You must assume this role when you write.

③ Keep an eye on this timer so you have enough time to properly plan, write, and edit your work.

④ This section will explain to whom you are writing.

⑤ You will have three or four things to do in your message.

Formatting Your Message

In Writing Task 1, you will be writing an email regarding day-to-day matters. Since you are expected to write 150–200 words, your response should include paragraphing and standard email conventions, including the five components shown below.

---

[i] Dear Team Members,

> i. GREETING

[ii] As you are all aware, we will be travelling to Calgary this November for a series of meetings. I have been directed to take charge of the trip so I am writing to share our travel plans and business goals.

> ii. OPENER

[iii] We will be attending the annual meeting for residential realtors and meeting individually with four of the biggest Calgary real estate companies while we are there. Some of you were on the Montreal trip last year, and you may remember what a great time we had at the gala dinner. There was an outstanding jazz band and the wine was flowing all evening!

> iii. BODY

In any case, we'll be travelling by plane, leaving on November 24 and returning November 28. I wish we could take the train because the scenery would be breathtaking and it would be a fun trip. However, the train takes 24 hours while the plane is just 1 hour, so obviously we'll have to fly.

In Calgary, we'll be staying downtown at the Palliser Hotel. This is one of the oldest buildings in the city and it's a four-star hotel, so we will be very comfortable and we'll be able to access local transportation very easily. The hotel has incredibly comfortable beds and an affordable pub, so we can continue our drinking traditions after our meetings. During our leisure time, it will be possible for us to relax without travelling far.

> iv. CLOSER

[iv] I look forward to another great business trip together!

[v] With best wishes,

> v. SIGN-OFF

Jake Harkness

> **Tip** Follow standard email format:
> - Add a comma after your Greeting and Sign-off.
> - Leave a line space before and after each paragraph, or indent 5 spaces
> - Stay on topic within each paragraph.

Notice how the Greeting and Opener are different:

GREETING: This is the salutation and it comes first.

OPENER: This "opens" the body of the email by introducing the reason for the message and getting the reader's attention. It comes at the beginning of the first paragraph.

The **BODY** makes up most of your message and comes between the Opener and the Closer. It contains your main points and supporting details.

The Closer and Sign-off both come at the end:

CLOSER: This "closes" the body of the email by summarizing what has been said and/or stating what kind of action or response the writer is hoping for. It comes at the end of the last paragraph.

SIGN-OFF: This comes after the body of the email and just before the writer's name. It ends the email.

A line space is used between all email components.

Activity 1

The writer of the test response below did not use correct email format. Without looking back at the example response, identify the components of the message by circling each of them. Rewrite the message so that you can create three paragraphs, change or add punctuation to the Greeting and Sign-off if required, and add line spaces where needed.

Dear Building Manager! I am writing to make a complaint about a problem that I am

currently experiencing in apartment 214. I'm sure you are aware of the no-dogs policy in

the building. Over the last week I have heard a dog barking at various times throughout the

day; however, it is loudest and most disturbing at night. I think that it sounds like the dog

is in the apartment next door to mine. If you could arrange to make a visit to the apartment

during the daytime, I am sure that you will see that there is a dog kept in the apartment

and then you could have a discussion with the renters about the dog's removal. I would be

grateful for your action on this matter as soon as possible, as it is disrupting my sleep and

my family's sleep as well. If this problem isn't resolved soon, I'm afraid that I'll have to

contact the local bylaw office. Sincerely

Relating Tone, Task, and Register

Tone

Tone is your attitude about the situation as expressed through your opinion and word choice. Your tone depends on whom you are writing to, why you are writing, and your intentions. You will need a good understanding of the situation to determine which tone is the most suitable.

Activity 2A

Look at the list of tones in the box below and decide whether they are positive or negative.

Respectful	Sarcastic	Optimistic	Helpful
Enthusiastic	Aggressive	Pessimistic	Co-operative
Critical	Insulting	Understanding	Angry
Complimentary	Arrogant	Defensive	Sincere

Negative Tone		Positive Tone	

Tone depends on the context. When the tone is inappropriate, it may mean that it is either too positive or too negative for the given situation. For the chart below, refer to Writing Task 1 on page 53 for the context. Below, you will see the thinking process of a higher-level test taker as he reviews three variations of a sentence. Look at how the sentences have been improved.

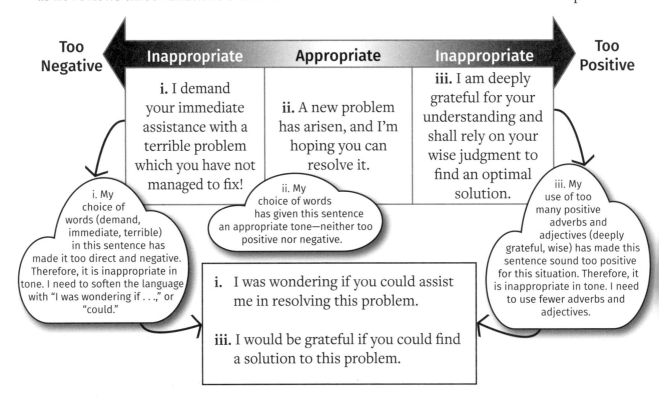

Activity 2B

Look at the email components below. First, identify if they are Openers or Closers on the left. Then, decide if the tone of each sentence is appropriate or inappropriate. The first one has been done for you.

EMAIL COMPONENT	OPENER/CLOSER	TONE
Closer	1. Thank you in advance for dealing with this issue.	*Appropriate*
	2. I am very sorry to bother you with a small problem related to a cute little dog.	
	3. I have an issue that I'm hoping you can solve.	
	4. I request that you make sure this dog stops being a disturbance today.	
	5. I expect to hear from you today with a satisfactory solution to this unbearable living situation.	

Activity 2C

Each sentence below has some problem language (which has been underlined) that makes it either too weak or too assertive. Fix each sentence by choosing a replacement word or phrase to make it appropriate for a formal situation.

1. If you really don't mind, I'm hoping that you can speak with the tenant about his dog.
   a) I would be ever so grateful if you would
   b) You have to
   c) I would appreciate it if you would

2. I expect you to deal with this as soon as possible.
   a) I will deal with this if you don't deal
   b) Thank you in advance for dealing
   c) Be sure that you deal

3. That horrible mutt shouldn't be living in this building.
   a) My neighbour's dog
   b) That insignificant little dog
   c) That disruptive beast

4. I most truly hope that you can find a solution to this problem.
   a) I look forward to finding
   b) It's imperative that you come up with
   c) I expect you to find

5. <u>I would be forever grateful for any help you can offer.</u>
    a) I'm sure you could definitely help me.
    b) I appreciate your assistance.
    c) I expect your immediate assistance.

6. <u>You had better be aware of the</u> pet policy in this building.
    a) As per our landlord/tenant agreement, there is a no-
    b) I expect that you have made yourself aware of the
    c) Has anyone told you about the

Task

You need a good understanding of the task before you start planning and writing. During the test, read the description and the instructions carefully to learn about the situation that you will be writing about. Keep these four "RASP" questions in mind:

ROLE:	What is my role in this task?
AUDIENCE:	Who is my audience?
SITUATION:	What is the situation?
PURPOSE:	What is the purpose of my email?

Your answers will help you decide which tone and register to use in your message, as well as what you need to say.

Activity 3

Look back at the Writing Task 1 example on page 53 to answer these questions.

1. What is the situation about?
    a) A problem with the building manager
    b) A problem with the cat next door
    c) A problem related to the no-dog policy

2. What role am I playing in this situation?
    a) An unhappy dog owner
    b) An unhappy renter
    c) The building manager

3. Who am I writing to?
    a) The building owner
    b) The neighbour
    c) The manager of the building

4. What is the purpose of the message?
    a) To complain about the person involved
    b) To find a solution to the problem
    c) To get the policy changed

Register

What level of formality should you aim for in your response? The level of formality—the register—is determined by your relationship with the recipient and the situation described in the task instructions.

	Informal		Level of Formality		Formal
	• Friend • Family member		• Colleague • Acquaintance	• Stranger	• Supervisor • Landlord

Activity 4

Answer these questions about the register and tone of the message for Activity 1 on page 55. Explanations are provided in the Answer Key.

> 1. What Greeting is the best choice for this email? Note, there is only one correct answer.
>   a) Dear Mr. Jackson,
>   b) Hey Mr. Jackson,
>   c) Respected Manager of 239 Oak Street,
>   d) To Whom It May Concern,
>
> 2. Choose the best way to begin your first paragraph.
>   a) You really must help me with an unbearable problem!
>   b) Are you aware that Jack in Suite 579 has a massive hairy dog that barks endlessly every single night?
>   c) I have no idea what I'm going to do if you can't help me deal with my neighbour.
>   d) I am a resident of 239 Oak Street and I'm writing about a problem related to the no-dog policy in this building.

Activity 5A

Decide if each component is formal (F), informal (INF), appropriate for both (B), or inappropriate (IA). Write the corresponding letter(s) to the left of each expression. Explanations have been provided in the Answer Key.

	GREETINGS		BODY		SIGN-OFFS
	Hey!		You obviously don't care.		TTYL
	Dear Mr. Snow,		I'd like to thank you.		Take care,
	Dear Jack,		With respect to the aforementioned problem,		Hugs!
	Dude!		And then there was the time		Regards,
	Your Eminence,		I would like to draw your attention to		Sincerely,
	To Whom It May Concern,		Have you noticed that		Yours most graciously,

Activity 5B

Add a Greeting, Body phrase, and Sign-Off from the chart on the previous page to match the tone of the email below. Then answer the questions under the message.

[1] ——————————

[2] —————————— the renter in Suite 215 is an idiot? This guy has some kind of really noisy dog that loves to bark in the middle of the night. All night, every night. Obviously this renter doesn't know how to read, because if he did he would surely know about the no-dog policy that is mentioned in our lease and posted next to our mailboxes.

I need you to do something about this right away—before I take matters into my own hands! I haven't slept in 2 weeks, since I moved into this building. And, by the way, I have some other complaints, too.

Anyway, I demand that you evict this guy from the building by tomorrow at noon. If you don't, I will contact the police immediately. And I will go talk to this dog owner myself and tell him what I think.

[3] ——————————,

Henry Giraldo

Suite 214

4. What is the level of formality in this message?
   a) Very formal
   b) Formal
   c) Informal
   d) Very informal

5. How would you categorize the tone of this message?
   a) Appropriate
   b) Inappropriate

6. Which attitudes best express the tone of the message? You may select up to two choices.

   ○ Angry
   ○ Sincere
   ○ Helpful
   ○ Critical
   ○ Pessimistic

Creating an Outline

An outline is your writing plan. It lists the main ideas and key supporting details in the order that you decide to write about them. Writers who take the time to draft an outline often produce a more organized, well-written, and clear response.

Time Management

Follow this recommendation to make sure you have enough time to organize, write, and revise your response:

OUTLINE	WRITE	EDIT
About 3 minutes	About 20 minutes	About 3 minutes

Notice that both tasks come with a built-in partial outline! Look at the Writing Task 1 sample below and see if you can spot this partial outline.

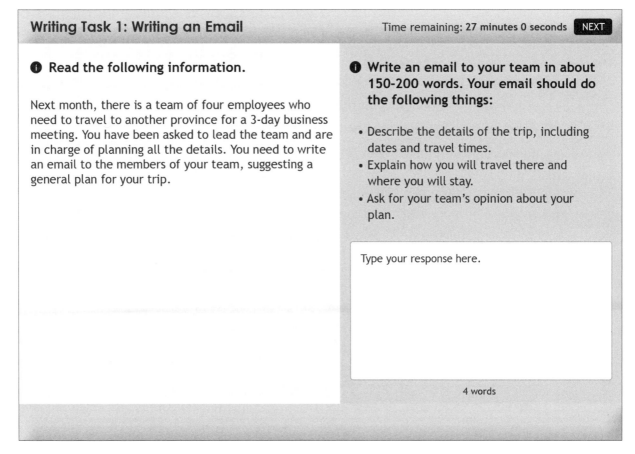

The partial outline is the bullet points on the right side of the page above the typing box. You also need to consider some elements from the description on the left to create a complete outline.

Outline Format

You are writing an email of 150–200 words, so you likely won't write more than two or three paragraphs. Refer to page 55 for the five components of an email message for Writing Task 1.

The Four-Step Outline Method

When you are practicing and preparing for the test, it is helpful to make notes as you work through the four steps in this method. Once you learn the method, you should be able to do most of the steps in your head during the official test.

STEP 1: Use your RASP questions from the Relating Tone, Task, and Register section of this module to gather all the basics. Refer back to the examples in that section to review this skill, and jot the answers on your notepaper before you start your outline. To save time, use abbreviations if you can. Abbreviations used in the example below are "bus." for "business" and "prov." for "province."

ⓘ Read the following information.

Next month, there is a [1] team of four employees who need to travel to another province for a 3-day business meeting. [2] You have been asked to lead the team and [1] are in charge of planning all the details. [3] You need to write an email to the members of your team, [4] suggesting a general plan for your trip.

1. **SITUATION:** Planning details for 3-day bus. trip to another prov.
2. **ROLE:** Leader of work team
3. **AUDIENCE:** Work team
4. **PURPOSE:** Suggest a plan

STEP 2: Next, use the bullet points from the Task 1 question to decide on the main points for your email, and jot these down as well. Abbreviations used in the example below are "incl." for "include" and "transp." for "transportation."

- Describe the <u>details of the trip</u>, including <u>dates</u> and <u>travel times</u>.
- Explain <u>how you will travel there</u> and <u>where you will stay</u>.
- <u>Ask</u> for your <u>team's opinion</u> about your plan.

MAIN POINTS:
1. Details, incl. dates and travel times
2. Transp. and hotels
3. Get team's input

STEP 3: Now look at your main points. Some may be simple and clear, but others may require supporting details. See if you can think of details to develop and/or support some of your main points.

STEP 4: Finally, look at your notes and arrange your main points into the most logical order. Select the best supporting details for each point and make sure these are also in a logical order.

Activity 6

Complete the outline below. Remember to put your main points in a logical order. Select the best two or three details for each point and put them in a logical order as well. You may use just two details to develop some points because your response should not be more than about 200 words.

Purpose of Message	Suggest a general plan for the trip and ask for each team member's opinion.
Opener	
Point 1	1. 2. 3.
Point 2	1. 2. 3.
Point 3	1. 2. 3.
Point 4	1. 2. 3.
Closer	

Activity 7

For practice in Writing Task 1 responses, use your outline to write a 150–200 word message in 20–25 minutes. If possible, type your response on a computer because that is what you will be doing during the CELPIP Test. When you are done, compare your response to the samples in the Answer Key. What are the similarities and differences between your response and the two samples?

Staying on Topic

Your email should communicate three or four ideas about the topic in a clear and focused way. Making sure that you are always on topic as you write your response will help with this. Every sentence in your response should relate directly to the purpose of your message. Remember that you should write about 150–200 words. If you go off topic, you run the risk of either not fully developing your main ideas, or exceeding the word count limit.

Activity 8

Read this response to the same Writing task and answer the questions.

Dear Team Members,

[1] As you are all aware, we will be travelling to Calgary this November for a series of meetings. [2] I have been directed to take charge of the trip, so I am writing to share our travel plans and business goals.

[3] We will be attending the annual meeting for residential realtors and meeting individually with four of the biggest Calgary real estate companies while we are there. [4] Some of you were on the Montreal trip last year, and you may remember what a great time we had at the gala dinner. [5] There was an outstanding jazz band and the wine was flowing all evening!

[6] In any case, we'll be leaving on November 24 and returning November 28 and travelling by plane. [7] I wish we could take the train because the scenery would be breathtaking and it would be a fun trip. [8] However, the train takes 24 hours while the plane is just 1 hour, so obviously we'll have to fly.

[9] In Calgary, we'll be staying downtown at the Palliser Hotel. [10] This is one of the oldest buildings in the city. It's a four-star hotel, so we'll be very comfortable and we'll be able to access local transportation easily. [11] The hotel has incredibly comfortable beds and an affordable pub, so we can continue our drinking traditions after our meetings. [12] During our leisure time it will be possible for us to relax without travelling far.

[13] I look forward to another great business trip together!

With best wishes,

Jake Harkness

249 words

Time Management

Watch the clock and your word count as you write! Make sure your response is at least 150 words before it's time to review and improve your work.

1. The response on page 64 is not completely on topic. Identify the sentences that should be removed because they do not directly support the topic.

○ 1   ○ 6   ○ 11
○ 2   ○ 7   ○ 12
○ 3   ○ 8   ○ 13
○ 4   ○ 9
○ 5   ○ 10

2. Which ideas should the writer add to fully develop the purpose of the message? Check all that apply.
   ○ Travel dates
   ○ Travel times
   ○ How they will travel
   ○ Where they will stay
   ○ Asking for their opinion

3. Using your notebook, follow these steps to rewrite the message and keep it on topic:
   • Remove the sentences that are off topic.
   • Add in the missing ideas.
   • Include additional information and reorganize part or all of the response to make it better.

Compare your edited version to the one in the Answer Key. Did you include all the required points and is your response now completely on topic?

Demonstrating Range of Vocabulary

Using vocabulary effectively is a key skill for both Writing tasks. One way to ensure that you demonstrate the full range of your vocabulary is to avoid repetition. The process of rephrasing ideas using different words is called paraphrasing. For instance, a paraphrase of "assessing your work" would be "checking your writing." In both cases, different vocabulary is used, but the meaning remains the same.

Try to avoid repeating words and phrases from the instructions; repeating isn't wrong, but paraphrasing better demonstrates your range of vocabulary. In addition to paraphrasing ideas from the test questions, you can do so with your own ideas.

Another way of showing your range of vocabulary is by using more precise language. Try to avoid vague, general descriptions in sentences—the more detail you can add, the better.

> **Tip**
> - Express your ideas accurately and precisely.
> - Use descriptive adjectives, strong verbs, and precise nouns.
> - Make sure the reader can easily understand your meaning.

Look at the Writing task, sample response, and explanation below to learn more about why restating ideas is a key test skill.

Writing Task 1: Writing an Email   Time remaining: 27 minutes 0 seconds   **NEXT**

ⓘ **Read the following information.**

You recently forgot your watch at the gym. The watch is important to you because it was a gift from your grandparents.

ⓘ **Write an email to the manager of your gym in about 150-200 words. Your email should do the following things:**

- Explain where you left the watch.
- Describe why it is important that you get your watch back.
- Explain how you may be contacted if the watch is found.

> Type your response here.
>
> 4 words

Hello Mr. Crofton,

My name is David Hill and I go to your gym on 10155 Sunhaven Street.

[1] **I am writing to you because I recently forgot my watch at the gym** and I think I left my watch in the fitness room. [2] **The watch is a Rolex watch and is red.** If the watch is not in the fitness room maybe I left it in the weight room.

First, the watch is very important for me because it was a gift from my grandparents. Also it is important because it was very expensive. So it is important that I get my watch back. [3] **You can contact me if the watch is found.** [4] **Contact me at my cellphone number: 604-123-4567.**

Thank you,

David Hill

125 words

Consider these problems related to this test taker's limited vocabulary:

- His response is only 125 words.
- He seems to rely on the wording in the question, except for a basic description of the watch and where it might be.
- His limited vocabulary also limits the ideas he can express. While he addresses all three bullet points, his ideas aren't very precise or detailed.
- He repeats key phrases from the test question (see the blue phrases).

Activity 9A

1. At 125 words, the response on page 66 is quite short. It could be improved by providing additional details that would develop the main ideas and demonstrate a wider vocabulary range. What other details could the writer include, without going off topic?
   a) A story about his grandparents
   b) Why his grandparents gave him the watch ✓
   c) Other important things he has lost
   d) How angry he will be if he doesn't get his watch back

Activity 9B

Look at the same response. For each numbered sentence, choose the best replacement.

1. a) I'm writing to you because last week I left my watch at the gym.
   b) I'm writing to you because that watch was a gift from my grandparents. ✗
   c) I'm pretty sure that I left my watch at the gym at some point.
   d) I think I lost my watch somewhere.

2. a) It is a Rolex watch. ✓
   b) The watch is red. ✓
   c) It is a red Rolex watch.
   d) The watch is both red, and it is a Rolex.

3. and 4. (These sentences can be combined to improve the writing style.)
   a) Get in touch with me as soon as possible at 604-123-4567. ✗
   b) If you find the watch, please phone or text me right away at 604-123-4567. ✓
   c) Please contact me when you find the watch at 604-123-4567.
   d) When you have the watch, call me please at 604-123-4567.

Activity 10A

For each general noun in the chart below, find up to three specific nouns/noun phrases that match. Add one more noun phrase to each list if you can. The first one has been done for you, and it includes an example of a noun phrase you could think of on your own.

SPECIFIC NOUNS / NOUN PHRASES			
~~watch band~~	~~fitness centre~~	~~change room~~	~~fitness lesson~~
~~grandfather~~	~~session~~	~~studio~~	practice space
~~weight training course~~	grandparent	~~leisure centre~~	~~timepiece~~
~~grandmother~~	~~wristwatch~~	health club	~~watch strap~~

GENERAL NOUNS	SPECIFIC NOUNS/NOUN PHRASES
class	1. *session* 2. *fitness lesson* 3. *weight training course* 4. *meditation class*
watch	1. Real watch timepiece 2. leather strap 3. wristwatch 4. watch band
area	1. change room 2. practice space 3. leisure centre 4. fitness centre
band	1. leather band 2. plastic band 3. steel band 4.
gym	1. studio 2. 3. 4.
person	1. grand father 2. grand mother 3. grand parent 4.

Activity 10B

For each common adjective in the chart below, find up to three descriptive adjectives/adjective phrases that match. Add one more adjective phrase to each list if you can. The first one has been done for you.

DESCRIPTIVE ADJECTIVES / ADJECTIVE PHRASES					
~~very costly~~	~~scarlet~~	~~highly significant~~	~~missing~~	of great consequence	~~high-priced~~
~~thoroughly miserable~~	~~after everything else~~	~~nowhere to be found~~	~~truly unhappy~~	~~completely vanished~~	~~essential~~
~~deep crimson~~	~~pricey~~	~~final~~	~~ruby~~	~~in the end~~	gloomy

COMMON ADJECTIVES	DESCRIPTIVE ADJECTIVES/ADJECTIVE PHRASES
red	1. *deep crimson* 2. *scarlet* (ecculate) 3. *ruby* (rubis) 4.
lost	1. missing 2. completely vanished (complètem. disparu) 3. nowhere to be found 4.
expensive	1. high-priced 2. pricey (chère) 3. very costly 4. expensive
important	1. essential 2. highly significant 3. 4.
last	1. final 2. in the end 3. after everything else 4.
sad	1. Truly unhappy gloomy (cafardeuse) 2. Thoroughly miserable 3. depressed 4. down

Activity 10C

For each weak verb in the chart below, find up to three strong verbs/verb phrases that match. Add one more verb phrase to each list if you can. The first one has been done for you.

STRONG VERBS / VERB PHRASES			
believe	misplace	retrieve	get in touch with
come across	phone me	have in my possession	be unable to find
give me a call	get a hold of	assume	own
obtain	get back	completely lose track of	suppose

WEAK VERBS	STRONG VERBS/VERB PHRASES
lose	1. *misplace* 2. *completely lose track of* 3. *be unable to find* 4.
find	1. 2. 3. 4.
call	1. phone me 2. get back 3. give me a call 4.
think	1. believe 2. suppose 3. assume 4.
get	1. obtain 2. Retrieve (Recuperer) 3. 4.
have	1. have in my possesion 2. own . 3. 4.

Activity 11

Here is another response to the test question on page 66. For each pair of underlined phrases, circle the phrase which provides more description, more specifics, or more information. As you make your choices, try not to select answers that include key words that have already been used in the response.

Dear Lifesource Gym Management,

I [1] was at/took a spin class at your gym last Friday evening, and when I got home, [2] I knew/I realized right away that [3] I had somehow forgotten/I left my watch there. I must have left it in the change room, as I usually [4] take it off/stow it safely away before going into the [5] hot yoga studio/room. My locker number is 57, and I believe the watch [6] should be there/is hidden away on the top shelf.

This watch [7] has great sentimental value/is important to me as it was a gift from my grandparents. My grandmother passed away last December and this is the [8] last thing/final gift she ever gave to me. [9] I'll be visiting/I'll see my grandfather [10] next week/soon, and he will without a doubt ask about the watch. [11] Therefore/As I hope you can see, it is very important that I get it back.

If you find the watch, please [12] contact me as soon as you possibly can/call me on my cell at 416-123-5678. If I miss your call, leave me a message and I'll definitely phone you right away.

Thank you!

Using Time Sequencers and Conjunctions

Time sequencers are useful when you write about a series of events, which you sometimes need to do for Task 1 of the Writing Test. Conjunctions are words or phrases used to join ideas together. Conjunctions are often used to join ideas within a sentence or to show how two sentences are related. These are both important features of a high-level email response. Appropriate use of time sequencers and conjunctions helps to produce a logical and coherent response, so readers can more easily understand the order of events as well as the relationship between ideas in your email or survey response.

Tip Balance your sentences! Use conjunctions to create long sentences with several related ideas—but make sure you include short sentences in your response as well. Short sentences are useful when you want to stress an important point.

Activity 12

Put each time sequencer into the correct group. There are four in each group.

after that	unexpectedly	finally	meanwhile	all of a sudden	after
when	3 hours later	to begin with	during	next	in 2 weeks
while	first	then	suddenly	firstly	in the end
without warning	lastly	first of all	at 2:00	next year	ultimately

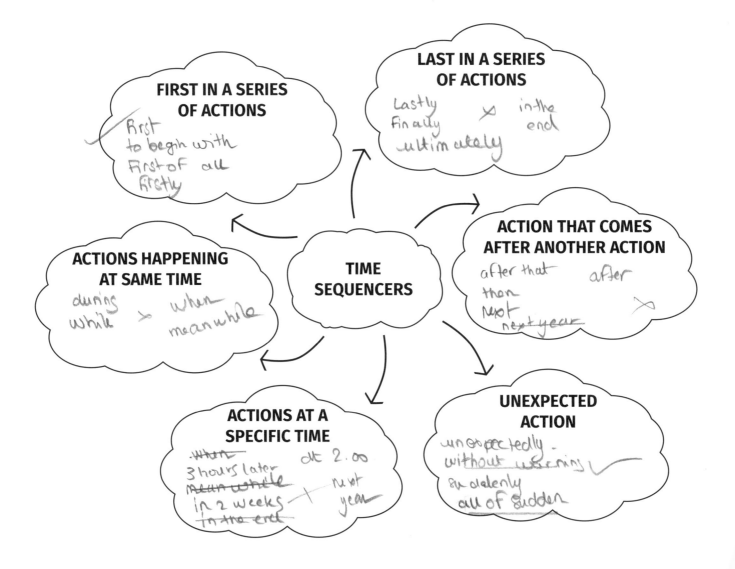

FIRST IN A SERIES OF ACTIONS

First
to begin with
First of all
firstly

LAST IN A SERIES OF ACTIONS

Lastly
Finally   in the end
ultimately

ACTIONS HAPPENING AT SAME TIME

during
while   when
meanwhile

TIME SEQUENCERS

ACTION THAT COMES AFTER ANOTHER ACTION

after that   after
than
Next
next year

ACTIONS AT A SPECIFIC TIME

3 hours later   at 2.00
meanwhile   next year
in 2 weeks
in the end

UNEXPECTED ACTION

unexpectedly
without warning
suddenly
all of sudden

Activity 13

Look at the test question and response below. Choose the correct time sequencers from the list of possible answers

---

Writing Task 1: Writing an Email   Time remaining: 27 minutes 0 seconds   NEXT

ⓘ Read the following information.

Next month, there is a team of four employees who need to travel to another province for a 3-day business meeting. You have been asked to lead the team and are in charge of planning all the details. You need to write an email to the members of your team, suggesting a general plan for your trip.

ⓘ Write an email to your team in about 150-200 words. Your email should do the following things:

- Describe the details of the trip, including dates and travel times.
- Explain how you will travel there and where you will stay.
- Ask for your team's opinion about your plan.

Type your response here.

4 words

---

at 2:00 p.m.	suddenly	next	the next morning
before	to begin with	after	meanwhile

Good evening team,

This email is to explain the details of our business trip.

[1] _To begin with_, we will be departing from Vancouver airport on Monday, September 3rd, at 7:00 a.m. and arriving in Toronto [2] _at 2 p.m._. Be sure to get to the airport at least 2 hours prior to the departure time.

[3] _Next_ we have picked up our luggage, our driver will be waiting for us at the pickup area on the arrivals level. [4] _After_, he will take us to the Western Hotel so we can drop off our suitcases and prepare for our 2-hour meeting starting at 4:00 p.m.

[5] meanwhile our clients will be assembling for that meeting in the Pacific Room at our hotel.

Upon completion of the meeting, we will head to the Cabana restaurant with our clients. The restaurant is located on the east side of the hotel lobby. [6] The next morning, after a well-earned sleep, we will assemble for breakfast at 7:30 [7] before leaving for the airport at 8:45 to catch our 11:00 a.m. flight.

If you [8] suddenly find yourself having to deal with any unforeseen events during this busy day, be sure to text me immediately.

Please let me know if you have any concerns or suggestions.

Thank you,

Julia Rowgen

Activity 14A

Match each conjunction on the left with its function on the right by joining them with a line.

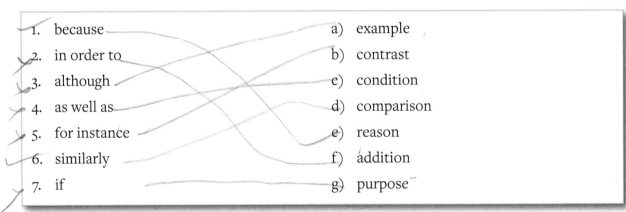

1. because   a) example
2. in order to   b) contrast
3. although   c) condition
4. as well as   d) comparison
5. for instance   e) reason
6. similarly   f) addition
7. if   g) purpose

Activity 14B

Decide if each sentence below is grammatically correct by circling ✓ (correct) or ✕ (incorrect). Remember that a conjunction needs to either join two ideas in one sentence or show how one sentence relates to the one that came before it.

1. Because we will have clients from eight companies at the meeting.   ✓ ⓧ
2. We have booked the meeting at the hotel so that we don't have to travel to get there.   ✓ ⓧ
3. In order to make this a success, we really need to deliver a quality presentation.   ✓ ✕
4. Although it seems very challenging.   ✓ ✕
5. As well as starting the dinner on time.   ✓ ⓧ
6. We need to make a positive impact on our clients. For instance, each team member could discuss their area of expertise.   ✓ ✕
7. Make sure you get to the airport 2 hours before our flight takes off; similarly, you should be at the airport 2 hours before the return flight.   ✓ ✕
8. If you encounter any problems during the trip, text me immediately.   ✓ ✕

Activity 15

Look at the Writing response below. For each pair of underlined conjunctions, choose the one that joins the ideas effectively. Consider which conjunction expresses the correct relationship between the two ideas, as well as which one fits grammatically into the sentence. The first one has been done for you.

Hello everyone,

As you all know, we have a business meeting in Vancouver next week. I am writing to present the plan for this trip.

I propose that we rent a car [1] if / because this is a comfortable and economical way to travel, and it gives us more freedom than flying from Calgary to Vancouver. [2] For instance / Although, we can stop at a few places along the way for sightseeing and meals. I was thinking of booking the Holiday Inn in Kelowna on Friday [3] so that / as well as we can take advantage of the good deals available online. [4] Because / Although the Holiday Inn offers good rates in Vancouver, as well, I feel we should stay at the Marriott, instead, because it has a better downtown location for our purposes.

Our conference starts Friday and ends Saturday. [5] ~~So that~~ / In order to be in top shape for our presentations, be sure to get a good sleep on Thursday night. [6] ~~As well as~~ / For instance making presentations, some of you will be doing one-on-one meetings with key clients, so be sure you have your updated meeting schedule before we leave. [7] ~~Because,~~ / Similarly, each of you is responsible for knowing when and where your presentations are taking place.

[8] ~~So that~~ / If you have any questions or concerns, contact me by noon tomorrow.

Sincerely,

Keizo

Correcting Your Errors

There are always ways to make your CELPIP Writing response better. Be sure to leave 3–4 minutes at the end of each Writing task to review and improve your work.

> **Tip** The Writing Test typing screen includes seven basic editing tools: cut, paste, copy, delete, undo, redo, and spell check. Make sure you are comfortable with these editing tools before you write the test.

When you are checking your work, try to think like a CELPIP Rater. Remember the four scoring categories (see the Writing Overview/back cover) and look for problems in those areas. Here is a checklist to help you review your work. If you are using this chart to check your practice responses, select (✓) "Yes" if you feel you have done something well, "Sometimes" if you have partially achieved a requirement, and "No" if you have missed a requirement.

CELPIP WRITING CHECKLIST	Yes	Sometimes	No
1. Is my meaning clear?			
2. Are the ideas organized logically?			
3. Have I rephrased key ideas?			
4. Have I chosen descriptive and precise words and phrases?			
5. Is my format correct?			
6. Do my paragraphs make sense?			
7. Have I used different sentence types and lengths?			
8. Are the tone and register appropriate?			
9. Have I used connecting words and phrases to connect ideas?			
10. Is each sentence complete?			
11. Have I minimized spelling, grammar, punctuation, and wording mistakes?			
12. Have I written 150–200 words?			

Be careful not to rely completely on spell check because it may not always notice a mistake (e.g., errors with words that sound the same, such as "there" and "their," usually aren't highlighted) and it may not always give you the correct word when it catches a mistake.

Look at this example:

> Try not to mape any mistakes when typing.

During the CELPIP Test, spell check would offer these choices:

- nape
- map
- ape

The correct word is "make," so in this case any test taker who selects one of the words offered by spell check will have a very obvious spelling mistake.

Activity 16

Look at the response to the test question shown below, and answer the questions that follow.

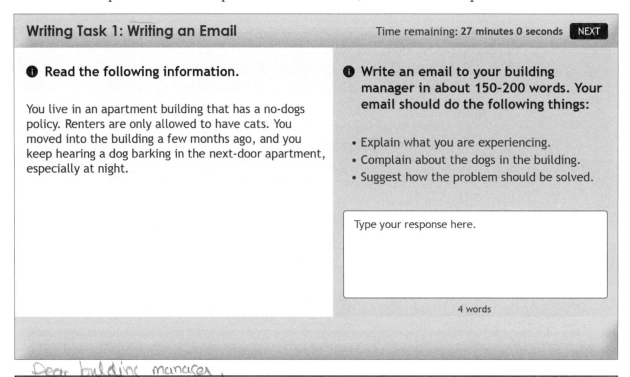

Writing Task 1: Writing an Email   Time remaining: 27 minutes 0 seconds   NEXT

ℹ **Read the following information.**

You live in an apartment building that has a no-dogs policy. Renters are only allowed to have cats. You moved into the building a few months ago, and you keep hearing a dog barking in the next-door apartment, especially at night.

ℹ **Write an email to your building manager in about 150-200 words. Your email should do the following things:**

- Explain what you are experiencing.
- Complain about the dogs in the building.
- Suggest how the problem should be solved.

Type your response here.

4 words

Dear building manager,

~~good day,~~

I live in apartement 705   *my next door neighbour.*

I am john, one of your tenants, and I have a problem with ~~your building~~. Every

evening when i am relaxing, *and* watching television, or eating my dinner, I ~~heard~~ a dog barking

in the next *door* ~~apartment~~. This is ~~distracting~~ *disturbing me*, especially at night when i am sleeping. i am

writing you ~~an email~~ *this* Because I do not want my neighbours to get mad at me when I talk to

them about their dog. *— please them regarding this matter*

Could you speak to ~~the~~ tenants in the next apartment about this, and

remind them that dogs are not allowed in the building? .

I wonder how a dog owner ended up living here, since this building has no-dog

policy? How come one of my neighbours has one. Please understand i'm not a dog hater, *but*

just want some real privacy and silence at night.

Can you visit my ~~tomorrow~~ neighbour and explain that dogs *are not* aren't allowed in the

building? Maybe you can help them *to* decide what to do about their dog. ?

~~hoping for your kind actions,~~ *I would be grateful for your action on this matter as soon as possible.*

John Parkdale

172 words

1. What are the two biggest problems in this response?
   a) Formatting and paragraphs c) Capitalization and punctuation
   b) Word count d) Sentence types

2. This test taker uses an appropriate tone, except in two places. Select the two sentences which the reader may find too direct.
   a) ... I have a problem with your building.
   b) ... I do not want my neighbours to get mad at me when I talk to them about their dog.
   c) How come one of my neighbours has one.
   d) I just want some real privacy and silence at night.

3. There are 14 grammar and/or punctuation mistakes in the Activity 16 response. Underline and correct each mistake.

Tip Always check your work for content/coherence, vocabulary, readability, and task fulfillment.

Activity 17

The response below has formatting and paragraph problems. Make any necessary formatting corrections and show where you would create paragraph breaks. For an extra challenge, fix any specific problems related to grammar, vocabulary, sentence structure, and tone.

Having moved into your building recently I was under the impression that there was a no-dogs rule.

However, each evening I can hear a dog barking in the next apartment and I am write to ask for your help with this! This is ridiculously unacceptable. Some nights I am awakened at 2:00 a.m. by the barking, and I find it challenging to focus at work the next day.

I am a doctor, it is important that I am always at my best for my patients. This building is near to my work, and also chose it specifically for the no-dogs rule, as I had problems in my previous apartment with dog noise, My badly sleeping was beginning to affect my work, and now the situation isn't any better since I'm having the same problems.

I know dogs are part of people's family, but would like you to sort out this problem. I'm not looking for a rent decrease. As this would not resolve the situation, but maybe I could move to another apartment away from the noise, or the person next door could move to another apartment.

187 words

Handwritten annotations: writing to you; problem/matter; that why I choose it specially for the; policy faced the same; am; It; be grateful if you can help me; with this issue

79

LEARNING FOCUS

- Steps for completing Task 2
- Choosing Option A or B
- Stating your opinion
- Supporting your opinion
- Selecting ideas
- Organizing ideas
- Using sentence variety
- Improving your work

In Writing Task 2: Responding to Survey Questions you are given background information about a survey question, two choices, and some specific instructions. Look at the infographic on the next page to learn more about these parts of the task. Before you start planning and writing, use the information in the description and instructions to decide on the approach, content, and tone of your message. Your purpose for Task 2 will always be the same: to express your position on the topic clearly and justify your choice with valid reasons.

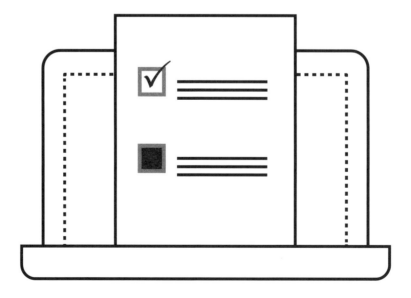

❶ Read the following information.

Discount Cards Survey

You work in a large general retail store. Your employer has decided to give discount cards to all its full-time employees. This will allow the staff to save money on goods in the store. The employer is asking your opinion on two discount card options.

❶ Choose the option that you prefer. Why do you prefer your choice? Explain the reasons for your choice. Write about 150-200 words.

○ Option A: I prefer a 20% discount on all products, **not** including groceries.

○ Option B: I prefer a 10% discount on all products, including groceries.

I prefer Option A because

5 words

1. Check survey title for information about topic.

2. Make sure you understand the situation.

3. Watch your time! Make your choice within first minute or two.

4. Choose one as quickly as you can. Leave time to plan and write your response.

5. Start with clear statement of your choice.

Steps for Completing Task 2

Read the instructions on both sides of the screen carefully. The two options and specific instructions on the right side of the screen are only half the story; you must understand the situation on the left side in order to make an informed choice and provide convincing reasons.

Activity 1

The list below gives all the steps for completing Task 2—but it is out of order. Number the steps to show how you should work through Writing Task 2. The last step has been completed for you.

#	STEPS TO COMPLETE TASK 2
6	Write and organize your response.
2	Scan the right side for specific information about the task and the two options.
4	Quickly decide which option you will write about.
3	Scan the left side to find the role, audience, and situation for the task.
5	Quickly create an outline.
1	Skim the instructions to get a general idea of what you need to do.
7	Edit and improve your response.

Activity 2

Read the instructions for the Discount Cards Survey on page 81 and select the correct answer choices in the chart below.

RASP: KEY INFORMATION IN THE TASK INSTRUCTIONS	ANSWER CHOICES
ROLE: I am . . .	a) a worker in a big store. _travailleur_ b) the employer in a big store. _employeur_
AUDIENCE: My reader(s) is/are . . .	a) the employees. b) my boss.
SITUATION: I must choose between . . .	a) 20% discount for everything except food **or** 10% discount on everything including food. b) 20% discount on groceries **or** 10% discount on groceries.
PURPOSE: My response should . . .	a) clearly explain the reasons for my choice. b) clearly explain why I want to save money.

Activity 3

Read this response to the Discount Cards Survey question and answer the question below.

> Thank you, manager, for this 20% discount on all products! I just bought a new house and I need to purchase a lot of furniture for my house.
>
> Right now I only have a dining table with four chairs and a bed frame. I was going to slowly purchase all the things I need over the coming year, but with this discount I can get things faster. I need a firm mattress, a 50″ TV and a 3-seater sofa. I hope I can get a loveseat to match my sofa too.
>
> All I can think about is getting my new house set up. It will be exciting for me once I buy all the things I need, and then I'll have a house-warming party. This will make me very happy!
>
> 130 words

Select each statement below in which the test taker followed the task instructions:

- She wrote as an employee at a big store.
- She wrote to her employer.
- She made a choice between the two options.
- She explained her choice.
- She gave several reasons for her choice.
- ☐ She wrote 150–200 words.

Choosing Option A or B

You may be tempted to write about the option you personally prefer, but this isn't always the best strategy. Use these guidelines to help you choose between the two options in Task 2:

- Try to quickly list at least three clear reasons to support each option (supporting reasons).
- Think of at least one good reason not to choose each option (reason against).
- Make sure your supporting reasons and your reasons against are factual, not emotional.

Which option did you find it easiest to write reasons for? That is the option you should write about. Before you start your response, try to list some useful vocabulary to support that viewpoint.

Activity 4

1. Refer to the Discount Cards Survey on page 81 and complete the following activity. Complete the chart below by listing supporting reasons, reasons against, and vocabulary.

	OPTION A I prefer a 20% discount on all products, **not** including groceries.	**OPTION B** I prefer a 10% discount on all products, including groceries.
Supporting Reasons	• Excellent savings • *more benificial* • *all products* •	• Benefits most employees since many of us buy our groceries here • • •
Reasons Against	• *need to buy food every week* *no furniture*	• Larger discount on other items would be appreciated
Vocabulary	• Greater savings • Household items • •	• Daily needs • One-stop shopping • Struggling to make ends meet •

2. How many supporting reasons did you list for each option?

Option A
- ○ 1
- ○ 2
- ○ 3
- ○ 4

Option B
- ○ 1
- ○ 2
- ○ 3
- ○ 4

When writing about your choice, try to remain objective—that is, try to base your writing on facts rather than feelings. If you have strong personal feelings about the option you choose, avoid overly emotional language. Your goal is to provide a convincing argument based on strong supporting details. Work on including precise and descriptive words and phrases.

évitu trop

Activity 5

Compare these two paragraphs from responses to the Discount Cards Survey and then answer the questions below.

A.   We all have to buy food every week, and therefore I choose Option B. It's totally obvious that every single employee of this company will be forever grateful to you for this opportunity to buy all our groceries cheaper. Just think of how happy my children will be when I bring them their favourite treats every week! It would be idiotic for us to take a larger discount on non-food items only—honestly, who can imagine not choosing a way to provide more food every week.

B.   Food is a necessity of life, and therefore I choose Option B. With this discount on all products, especially food, we can benefit from convenient one-stop shopping. All employees can efficiently and affordably provide for the daily needs of ourselves and our families. We can shop right after work and have more time to rest and relax, resulting in more productive employees. Some of us may even experience less stress at home because we will be able to provide the things our family members need.

1. Paragraph A contains overly emotional language, resulting in an inappropriate tone. Select the phrases that make this explanation unsuitable:
   ○ We all have to buy food every week.
   ○ It's totally obvious that every single employee of this company will be forever grateful . . .
   ○ It would be idiotic . . .
   ○ . . . take a larger discount on non-food items only
   ○ Honestly, who can imagine . . .

2. Paragraph B makes five main points and uses an appropriate tone. The five main points are:
   • Everyone needs food.
   • Employees can buy everything they need in one place.
   • Employees can shop after they finish their shift.
   • Employees will have more leisure time.
   • Employees will be more productive at work.

   What makes these points persuasive?
   a) Each one presents factual information.
   b) They are each about food.
   c) They show how much the writer cares about his family.

Activity 6

Look at the new Task 2 question and fill in the chart below.

Writing Task 2: Responding to Survey Questions
Time remaining: 26 minutes 0 seconds **NEXT**

ℹ **Read the following information.**

Parking or Bike Lane Survey

You live in an old neighbourhood in the city where cars can park on both sides of the street. Recently, cyclists have asked the local government to replace the parking spaces on one side of the street with a bike lane. This means that cars can park on only one side and only bikes can use the other side. The government has asked you to respond to an opinion survey.

ℹ **Choose the option that you prefer. Why do you prefer your choice? Explain the reasons for your choice. Write about 150-200 words.**

○ Option A: I think the city should replace parking spaces on one side of the street with a bike lane.

○ Option B: I think the city should keep parking spaces on both sides of the street.

Type your response here.

4 words

	OPTION A Replace parking spaces on one side of the street with a bike lane	OPTION B Keep parking spaces on both sides of the street
Supporting Reasons	• • • •	• • • •
Reasons Against	•	•
Vocabulary	• • • •	• • • •

Test Practice

Write a response to the Parking or Bike Lane Survey question. Give yourself about half an hour to complete this activity. Justify your choice with logical and well-supported reasons. You can compare your response to the Level 12 responses in the Answer Key.

Stating Your Opinion

Your Task 2 response should have a clear statement of your opinion within the first few sentences. Look again at the Parking or Bike Lane Survey task on the previous page, and read the following two samples.

> From my perspective, it makes good sense to exchange parking spaces for a bike lane on all the streets in our neighbourhood. This will impact positively on the residents of our neighbourhood for three reasons. First of all . . .

> I think the city should replace parking spaces on one side of the street with a bike lane. This makes good sense and will benefit many residents for the following three reasons. To start with . . .

Both examples clearly state the writer's opinion at the beginning and inform the reader that there will be three supporting reasons, but there is one difference. The first writer paraphrased her option choice by using her own words. The second writer, on the other hand, failed to rephrase Option A when stating his opinion. By repeating the wording from the question, this test taker has missed an opportunity to demonstrate his range of vocabulary.

Ideally, your statement of opinion should include these two features:

- A phrase indicating that you are about to express your opinion
- A restatement of the option you have chosen

Activity 7

1. Look at the two examples above and copy the phrases each writer has used to show they are going to state their opinion:

   a) _____

   b) _____

2. Look at the two examples above and copy the way each writer restated the option from the survey:

   a) _____

   b) _____

> **Tip** It is acceptable to make up statistics or evidence to support your opinion in the CELPIP Test. If you do this, try to make it sound believable. You can also support your opinion by claiming to be an expert on the topic through experience or education.

Supporting Your Opinion

You need to support your opinion with logical reasons, relevant information, and perhaps an example or story that strengthens your viewpoint.

Check that each idea you have chosen directly supports your choice by asking yourself these questions:

- How does this idea provide evidence or support for my opinion?
- What details can I add to develop this idea?
- How relevant are these details to my opinion on this topic?

Look at the Coffee Payment Survey question below and read the first paragraph from a sample response that follows.

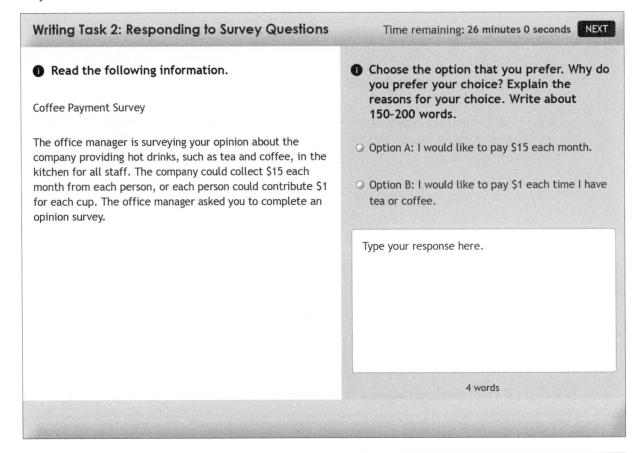

| Writing Task 2: Responding to Survey Questions | Time remaining: 26 minutes 0 seconds NEXT |

ⓘ **Read the following information.**

Coffee Payment Survey

The office manager is surveying your opinion about the company providing hot drinks, such as tea and coffee, in the kitchen for all staff. The company could collect $15 each month from each person, or each person could contribute $1 for each cup. The office manager asked you to complete an opinion survey.

ⓘ **Choose the option that you prefer. Why do you prefer your choice? Explain the reasons for your choice. Write about 150–200 words.**

○ Option A: I would like to pay $15 each month.

○ Option B: I would like to pay $1 each time I have tea or coffee.

Type your response here.

4 words

I would like to pay $1 each time I have tea or coffee. I love tea and I am very happy that the company will do this for us. This means that I can enjoy tea whenever I want and this will make me feel so good. Drinking tea at the office will make me feel appreciated and will help me relax. And this will make me a more productive worker.

There is one main problem with this paragraph in terms of how the writer supports her opinion:

- The writer has not provided any direct support for her choice.

The ideas in this paragraph all support how much the writer likes tea and how she feels that drinking tea will make her a better employee. While this is a good point, it is not relevant to why she wants to pay $1 per cup instead of $15 per month. This response, therefore, will lose points for Content/Coherence and Task Fulfillment (see the four categories for scoring on page 50).

The writer could improve her opening paragraph by adding more relevant ideas to support her opinion, such as these:

- I have a hot drink at the office just once or twice a week.
- I know that most of the employees rarely buy a coffee or tea.

Each idea provides strong support for why paying $1 per cup is a better choice by showing that most employees, including the writer, are probably spending under $10 per month.

Additionally, keep in mind that this writer simply repeats her chosen option in her response, without paraphrasing it. If she had used different words here, she could have better demonstrated her range of vocabulary.

One useful tool for deciding on an option and listing ideas to support your opinion is a mind map. A mind map is a visual way of organizing ideas. The main idea is usually in the middle, with branches leading to supporting ideas. Here is an example of a mind map for Option A.

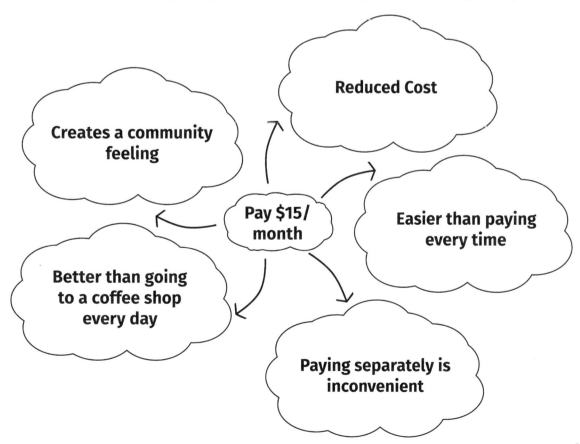

Activity 8

Use the mind map below to list ideas to support Option B. Try to come up with at least four ideas.

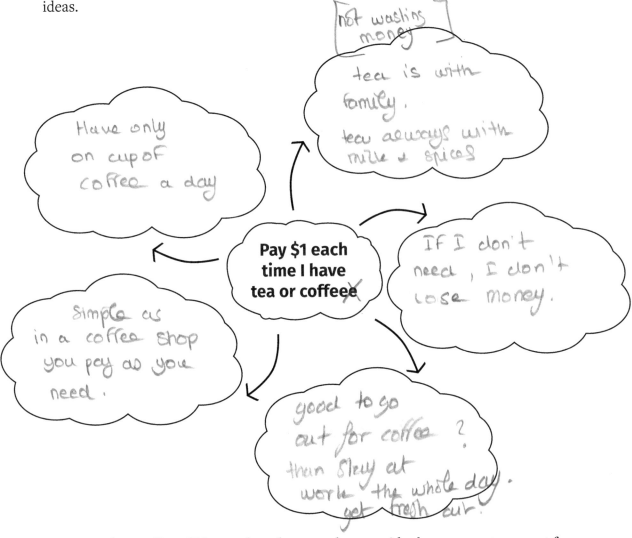

not wasting money

tea is with family.
tea always with milk + spices

Have only on cup of coffee a day

IF I don't need, I don't lose money.

Pay $1 each time I have tea or coffee~~e~~

Simple as in a coffee shop you pay as you need.

good to go out for coffee? than stay at work the whole day. get fresh air!

Once you have a list of ideas, select the ones that provide the strongest support for your opinion. You should include at least two main ideas in your response, and provide good supporting details for each one. It is not advisable to include more than three main ideas because you will not be able to support each one effectively.

Tip Watch for ideas that are too similar. If your ideas are very closely related, it might seem as if you have just one idea in your response.

Selecting Ideas

Once you have decided which option to write about and thought of some good supporting reasons, work on preparing a coherent response. When organizing your work, eliminate poor supporting ideas; they may weaken your response.

Work towards having about four reasons to choose from. Depending on how you choose

Option A or B, these may be in a mind map or in point form on your notepaper. Use these guidelines to help you choose your ideas:

- Make sure each idea directly supports your opinion.
- Choose ideas that aren't too similar.
- Select two or three ideas with good supporting details.
- Think of at least two details to support each idea if you can.

Look again at the ideas in the mind map for Option A on page 89. Here is the thinking behind how one test taker might choose his three strongest points.

REASON FOR OPTION A	TEST TAKER'S THINKING
Reduced cost	"I can prove that I will save money by showing how I would have to spend at least $1 per day on the other plan. Then I can talk about how others who drink this much will also like this plan." • Costs about $20 per month if we buy one cup per day • Cold Edmonton winters: most employees have more hot drinks and spend more
Easier than paying every time	"Many people don't carry cash nowadays. I can say that some employees may not be able to buy a tea or coffee when they want to if they have no money. Hmm, this seems closely related to the next topic and even the first topic, so I probably won't use it."
Paying separately is inconvenient	"I'll write about the convenience of paying just once a month and how frustrating it could be if employees need cash every time we want a coffee (Option B). This topic could be more interesting than the related one above." • I don't carry cash. • One monthly payment is more convenient. • I can have coffee whenever I want if I don't have to pay each time.
Better than going to a coffee shop every day	"This idea seems related to the first one about cost. I would have to compare the cost of going to a coffee shop to this payment plan and I think it might be repetitive, so no point in using it."
Creates a community feeling	"I can focus on how the monthly payment plan helps us all feel treated equally by the company." • Everyone is treated the same. • Everyone can benefit. • Employees will socialize in the coffee room regularly.

Now that the test taker is thinking more carefully about his ideas, he is able to provide better details to support the best ones. In the list below, notice that the ideas that seem similar to other stronger ones have now been left out.

OPINION: Pay $15 each month.
IDEA 1: REDUCED COST
* Costs about $20 per month if we buy one cup per day
* Cold Edmonton winters: most employees have more hot drinks and spend more
IDEA 2: PAYING SEPARATELY IS INCONVENIENT
* Encourages people to use the plan regularly
* Monthly plan removes possibility of feeling penalized for not having cash
* Supports regular socialization
IDEA 3: CREATES A COMMUNITY FEELING
* Fosters a sense of community
* Encourages participation
* Increases socialization at work, which could improve productivity

Activity 9

Look at the mind map you made for Activity 8 on page 90. Select the three best ideas and list supporting details for each of them.

OPINION: Pay $1 each time I have tea or coffee.

IDEA 1:_____
* _____
* _____

IDEA 2:_____
* _____
* _____

IDEA 3:_____
* _____
* _____

Tip Choose ideas or reasons that directly support your opinion and for which you can think of relevant supporting details.

Organizing Ideas

You now need to put your two or three best ideas into a logical order. When you take the time to do this, the reader will be able to follow your ideas easily and understand how they are related. Once again, here is the test taker's original order of ideas, presented in the order he thought of them.

OPINION: Pay $15 each month.
IDEA 1: REDUCED COST
- Costs about $20 per month if we buy one cup per day
- Cold Edmonton winters: most employees have more hot drinks and spend more

IDEA 2: PAYING SEPARATELY IS INCONVENIENT
- Encourages people to use the plan regularly
- Monthly plan removes possibility of feeling penalized for not having cash
- Supports regular socialization

IDEA 3: CREATES A COMMUNITY FEELING
- Fosters a sense of community
- Encourages participation
- Increases socialization at work, which could improve productivity

To organize his ideas more logically, our test taker decides to start with his last idea because he feels it will grab the reader's attention. He has also noticed that one point in his last idea (**increases socialization at work**) links to a detail (**supports regular socialization**) in his **paying separately** idea. Our test taker quickly reviews his details and changes the order in the **paying separately** idea to create more logical support. He feels it makes sense to end with the **reduced cost** idea because this presents a simple mathematical reason for why the monthly plan makes better sense and is a tidy way to complete his argument. His notes now look like this:

OPINION: Pay $15 each month.
IDEA 1: CREATES A COMMUNITY FEELING
- Fosters a sense of community
- Encourages participation
- Increases socialization at work, which could improve productivity

IDEA 2: PAYING SEPARATELY IS INCONVENIENT
- Supports regular socialization
- Monthly plan removes possibility of feeling penalized for not having cash
- Encourages people to use the plan regularly

IDEA 3: REDUCED COST
- Costs about $20 per month if we buy one cup per day
- Cold Edmonton winters: most employees have more than one hot drink per day and spend more

Our test taker is satisfied that his ideas and details are in a logical order. Now that he is ready to draft his response, he can focus on his writing skills because he has already decided what he will write about and how to organize his ideas.

Tip You may be able to improve your score by including one or two sentences about why the other option isn't a good choice.

Test Practice

Go back to your notes from Activities 8 and 9 for Option B. On a piece of notepaper, put your ideas and details into a logical order. Using your notes, write your own response. Compare your response to the Level 12 responses in the Answer Key for both Option A and Option B.

Using Sentence Variety

A good writing response features sentences that vary in length and type. Using a combination of simple, compound, and complex sentences helps writers indicate which ideas are more important and how ideas are related to each other. Writers who use different types of sentences have a better chance of expressing their ideas smoothly and achieving a higher level of coherence.

This chart provides a quick review of the key grammar terms we need to use when we talk about sentence variety.

GRAMMAR REFRESHER! Independent clauses are <u>underlined</u>. Dependent clauses are **bolded**. Conjunctions, transitions, and linking phrases are *italicized*.		
Term	**Definition**	**Example**
Independent Clause	A group of words with a subject and a verb that expresses a complete thought and can be a sentence.	<u>I like coffee.</u>
Dependent Clause	A group of words with a subject and a verb that does not express a complete thought and is not a complete sentence.	***because* I like coffee**
Simple Sentence	A sentence that has only one independent clause.	<u>I like coffee.</u> <u>Juice is good for my health.</u>
Compound Sentence	A sentence that has two or more independent clauses.	<u>I like coffee,</u> *but* <u>juice is better for my health.</u>
Complex Sentence	A sentence that has one independent clause and at least one dependent clause.	***When* I learned that juice is better for my health,** <u>I stopped drinking coffee.</u>
Compound-Complex Sentence	A sentence that has at least two independent clauses and at least one dependent clause.	<u>I like coffee,</u> *but* <u>I gave it up</u> ***because* juice is better for my health.**

Using Short and Simple Sentences

Refer again to the Coffee Payment Survey question on page 88. Then look at this paragraph from a response.

I would like to pay $15 per month. I drink a lot of coffee at work. Other people drink a lot of coffee or tea as well. It helps keep us awake. It helps us get things done. Most of us have at least one cup of coffee or tea each day. There are at least 20 days of work in a month. The $1 per coffee option would cost each of us upwards of $20 a month. The $15 per month option would be cheaper. It would encourage people to drink more coffee. Drinking more coffee would boost overall productivity. I hope our company will offer the $15 per month option. It would allow us to save money. We could also work harder.

This writer relies completely on simple sentences. Since each simple sentence presents one idea, it is challenging for the reader to know which ideas are more important.

Using a Variety of Sentence Types

Look at the edited response below to see how the writer could improve this paragraph.

I would like to pay $15 per month. **Like** everyone else, I drink a lot of coffee at work. It helps keep us awake **and** get things done. Most of us have at least one cup of coffee or tea each day, **and** there are at least 20 days of work in a month; **therefore,** the $1 per coffee option would cost each of us upwards of $20 a month. **In contrast**, the $15 per month option would not only be cheaper, it would encourage people to drink more coffee, **thus** boosting overall productivity. **In view of these factors,** I hope our company will offer the $15 per month option, **which** would allow us to save money **and** work harder.

Notice how this writer uses a variety of linking words and phrases (in blue) to express how each idea relates to the one before or after. This helps the reader know which ideas are most important. In addition, the changing sentence length and structure helps the reader stay interested and involved.

You can use conjunctions and linking words or phrases to show how the next idea relates to the one you just wrote about. See the chart on the next page for several different categories of linking words and phrases.

LINKING WORDS AND PHRASES		
SEQUENCE	**COMPARISON**	**CONTRAST**
to start with,	similarly,	although
in addition,	likewise,	on the other hand,
moreover,	similar to	on the contrary,
another/also	just as	in contrast to
lastly,/finally,	correspondingly,	conversely,
RESULT	**REASON**	**EXAMPLE**
as a result,	because	for example,
consequently,	since	for instance,
therefore,	so	such as
due to	so that	namely,
accordingly,	in order that	including

Activity 10

For each set of sentences below, create one compound or complex sentence using several conjunctions and/or linking words and phrases. You may make small grammatical changes (word form, adding or taking away a few words, etc.) so long as you don't change the meaning. The first one has been done for you.

it follows that	than	by	and results in
because	which	since	when
and	as a result	because	

1. Most employees drink two coffees a day.
   They work 5 days per week.
   They pay $10 per week for coffee.

   Since most employees drink two coffees a day and work 5 days per week, it follows that they pay $10 per week for coffee.

2. I would like to pay $15 per month.
   It is more convenient.
   I don't need to pay with cash.

   _____

   _____

3. It can be irritating to pay each time.
   This may distract us from our work.
   We may worry about having cash.

   _____

   _____

4. It will reduce my coffee expenses.
   It will help me save money.
   I consume a lot of coffee every day.

   _____

   _____

5. This plan makes coffee and tea affordable.
   It increases social interaction for the staff.
   It will make the employees happy.

   _____

   _____

Activity 11

Now you will practice linking simple sentences within the context of a response to Task 2. Read the response on the next page to the Parking or Bike Lane Survey question, and complete the response by selecting a suitable linking word or phrase from the chart.

Writing Task 2: Responding to Survey Questions   Time remaining: 26 minutes 0 seconds   **NEXT**

ⓘ Read the following information.

Parking or Bike Lane Survey

You live in an old neighbourhood in the city where cars can park on both sides of the street. Recently, cyclists have asked the local government to replace the parking spaces on one side of the street with a bike lane. This means that cars can park on only one side and only bikes can use the other side. The government has asked you to respond to an opinion survey.

ⓘ Choose the option that you prefer. Why do you prefer your choice? Explain the reasons for your choice. Write about 150-200 words.

○ Option A: I think the city should replace parking spaces on one side of the street with a bike lane.

○ Option B: I think the city should keep parking spaces on both sides of the street.

Type your response here.

4 words

---

that	consequently	when	although
as a result	for example	because	
similarly	to start with	another	

I believe that replacing parking spaces on one side of the street with a bike lane is more convenient.

[1] _____, I am sure that most residents would agree [2] _____ maintaining parking lanes on both sides of the street is a waste of space [3] _____ there are few visitors in our residential neighbourhood. [4] _____, many of our residents aren't drivers and [5] _____ they don't need to park on the street.

[6] _____ key factor is safety for cyclists, [7] _____ the majority of Calgarians don't think about this. Many of our residents are cyclists and [8] _____, we are concerned for our well-being [9] _____ cycling in our neighbourhood. Installing a bike lane should reduce the possibility of accidents involving cars and bicycles. [10] _____, I recently heard about a car accident on my street which claimed a life.

Let's put safety before convenience. Let's put people before cars! I look forward to having bike lanes in our neighbourhood soon.

Tip Using only long, complex sentences can be a mistake! Sometimes using short, simple sentences is an effective way to emphasize a key point, as shown in the last paragraph above.

Improving Your Work

In Writing Task 2 you need to write a persuasive argument to support your opinion. You also need to pay attention to other things including your vocabulary choices, format, tone, register, grammar, spelling, punctuation, sentence variety, and word count. There are many things to think about during the Writing Test, and it is difficult to get them all right on the first try! Devoting a few minutes to reviewing your response and making it better before your task time is up can actually make a difference.

When you review your work during the test, keep in mind the Writing Checklist from Unit 7 (this is repeated on the next page), and add these questions for Task 2:

- Have I expressed my opinion clearly?
- Have I provided at least two logical reasons to justify my choice?
- Have I supported each reason with relevant details?

Activity 12

Look again at the Discount Cards Survey question below and answer the questions about the sample response.

Writing Task 2: Responding to Survey Questions   Time remaining: 26 minutes 0 seconds   **NEXT**

ⓘ **Read the following information.**

Discount Cards Survey

You work in a large general retail store. Your employer has decided to give discount cards to all its full-time employees. This will allow the staff to save money on goods in the store. The employer is asking your opinion on two discount card options.

ⓘ **Choose the option that you prefer. Why do you prefer your choice? Explain the reasons for your choice. Write about 150-200 words.**

○ Option A: I prefer a 20% discount on all products, **not** including groceries.

○ Option B: I prefer a 10% discount on all products, including groceries.

> Type your response here.

4 words

Hi,

The first thing is I am really thankful to you for giving me a discount offer and time to choose from two. I want to choose the 10% discount on all products, including groceries. The main reason to choose this option is that I have a large family. My mom and dad live with me and I have three kids. I have a lot of family nearby. On weekends lots of people come to my home. My wife really likes to invite family for lunch or dinner and she wants to serve them homemade food. I need a lot of food.

I checked my shopping bills from the last three months. My food bill is more than other purchases. The kids eat a lot of food so we buy food every day. I think this is more important than other products. We need other products just once in a while, so give me 10% discount on all products.

Thanks a lot.

162 words

1. When this test taker reviews his response, will he answer "Yes" or "No" to each of these questions? After you answer, read the explanations in the Answer Key.
   a) Have I expressed my opinion clearly?
   b) Have I provided at least two logical reasons to justify my choice?
   c) Have I supported each reason with relevant details?

2. Look at the Writing Checklist and think about this response. Which answers should be "No"?

CELPIP WRITING CHECKLIST			
	Yes	Sometimes	No
1. Is my meaning clear?			
2. Are the ideas organized logically?			
3. Have I rephrased key ideas?			
4. Have I chosen descriptive and precise words and phrases?			
5. Is my format correct?			
6. Do my paragraphs make sense?			
7. Have I used different sentence types and lengths?			
8. Are the tone and register appropriate?			
9. Have I used connecting words and phrases to connect ideas?			
10. Is each sentence complete?			
11. Have I minimized spelling, grammar, punctuation, and wording mistakes?			
12. Have I written 150–200 words?			

Activity 13

Here is a higher-level response for the same test question. Answer the questions and read the explanations in the Answer Key.

> I would prefer the 10% option as I do all my shopping including groceries over the year from yours company. Working it out over a twelve month period for me to take the 20% discount which does not include groceries would mean that i would either be purchasing my groceries from another store at a higher cost to myself. Which when you think if i accept the lower percentage on all products including groceries I would be saving quite a reasonable amount financially and that your company would still be making an annual profit through my continued purchasing within the store.
>
> I feel it is better for both you as a company and myself as a customer to have a smaller percentage over the whole range of products than a higher percentage on all products except groceries. I look forward to a continued customer employer bond that will continue for many years
>
> 151 words

1. Which things does this test taker handle well?
   a) Vocabulary
   b) Sentence variety
   c) Tone and register
   d) All of the above

Now go back to the response and fix the three big problem areas of format, capitalization and punctuation, and reasons. Try to fix problems with sentence structure as well. Then check your response with the edited version in the Answer Key.

READING – UNIT 1

Activity 1

    1. B   2. A   3. C

Activity 2

1. Specific details

Explanation: To answer this question, you need to look for a particular detail in the message: what happened in October.

2. General meaning

Explanation: To answer this question, you need to quickly read over the message to get a general understanding of what the writer's main purpose is.

3. Inferring

Explanation: To answer this question, you need to draw conclusions based on what happened to Judith. Judith has stated that she won't be taking any more vacations with SunTime, so choices (a) and (b) are wrong. It is unlikely that knowing the name of the tour guide will satisfy Judith, so choice (d) is not a logical option. Choice (c) makes sense because Judith will probably feel satisfied if she gets some money back along with an apology.

READING – UNIT 2

Activity 1

    1. 11 minutes

    2. 3 sections

    3. 11 questions

    4. Roughly 45 seconds

Activity 2A

1. Tracey	6. B
2. Janice	7. A
3. A	8. D
4. C	9. Tracey is Janice's employee.
5. B	10. Tracey is requesting a leave of absence from work.

Activity 2B

1. B

Explanation: The phrase on the first line, "glad to hear," indicates that the author is happy about what he has heard. "Holiday" is mentioned later on this line, so it is likely that the author is glad that the reader is going on holiday.

2. D

Explanation: The first paragraph starts with "difference between motels and hotels," which indicates that the author will be discussing the differences in this paragraph. Also, key terms like "prefer a motel" and "instant exit" indicate reasons for a preference between the two. Note, however, that it is unclear whether this preference is the author's or the reader's.

3. D

Explanation: The second paragraph starts with the imperative statement "do some research," and this is followed by "where to stay." This indicates that the author wants to give some suggestions. He has included key terms like "websites," "travel guides," and "written reviews," which means he is suggesting that the reader go to those resources for more research. Towards the end of the paragraph, you can see key terms like "complaining," "bedbugs," and "unclean bathrooms"—these indicate that the writer is warning the reader against possible problems that he needs to be aware of.

Activity 3

1. Option (a) is the correct answer because the repeated phrase "ground floor" (see Lines 2 and 5) tells us that most motels only have one floor. While the things in the other options are referred to in the text, none

of them are correct because the specific aspects of options (b), (c), and (d) are not mentioned.

2. You should be able to determine option (c) is correct by first locating the word "managers" on Line 7, which tells you that the information you need is nearby. The phrase "a five-star rating means the highest quality" relates strongly to answer choice (c).

3. This paragraph contains information about amenities that the hotel has to offer, and the extra fees that may be charged for these amenities. In the final sentence of the paragraph, Marcel recommends that his friend call the hotel or motel directly for additional information. From this, you should be able to determine option (a) is correct. "Make inquiries" has a similar meaning to "additional information," while the other options do not match the information given in this paragraph.

Test Practice

1. A	4. B	7. D	10. D
2. C	5. A	8. C	11. D
3. C	6. D	9. A	

READING – UNIT 3

Activity 1A

1. traditional (see Barbara's Best Bakery, point 1)
2. voted (see Olia's Online Occasions, point 1)
3. reasonable (see Theresa's Tastiest Treats, point 5)
4. guaranteed (see Wanda's Wonderful Weddings, point 1)
5. unbeatable (see Theresa's Tastiest Treats, point 1)

Activity 1B

1. Barbara's Best Bakery
2. Wanda's Wonderful Weddings
3. Theresa's Tastiest Treats
4. Olia's Online Occasions
5. Theresa's Tastiest Treats

Activity 1C

1. Wanda's Wonderful Weddings—they offer vegan, nut-free, and gluten-free options.
2. Barbara's Best Bakery—they use red roses and ribbons.
3. Olia's Online Occasions—they will follow the theme of your choice.
4. Theresa's Tastiest Treats—they state they have reasonable prices but they don't give any examples.

Activity 1D

1. Olia's Online Occasions: voted most popular; offers tastings; themed cakes.
2. Wanda's Wonderful Weddings: serves 25–50 guests, which is good for a small guest list; vegan, nut-free, and gluten-free cheesecake would work for their families' dietary needs.

Activity 1E

1. B

Explanation: The key word here is "gluten-free." The cheesecake made by Wanda's Wonderful Weddings is the only option that mentions this term, so "cheesecake" must be the correct answer.

2. D

Explanation: The key terms here are "July," "topping," and "lemon cake." Strawberries ripen in the summer, and berries are a possible topping for the lemon cake made by Theresa's Tastiest Treats, so "local strawberries" must be correct.

3. C

Explanation: The answer is likely not Theresa's from the previous question, and Barbara's Best Bakery seems to serve the largest number of people. Therefore, "Barbara's" must be correct.

4. D

Explanation: Barbara's appears to be the only bakery that uses roses; therefore, "Barbara's Best Bakery" is correct.

5. D

Explanation: Alice's previous statement was about Barbara's Best Bakery. It is now being compared to a "themed cake." For a comparison like this, "On the other hand," fits most appropriately.

6. A

Explanation: Alice mentions Alan near the beginning of the message. Since the subject is wedding cakes, "Alice's fiancé" is the most likely answer.

7. B

Explanation: Near the beginning of the message, Alice mentions that her mother has researched wedding cakes already and has made "a list of four cake possibilities." Since the rest of Alice's message discusses these four possibilities, it is likely that Alice thinks her mother has been helpful.

8. B

Explanation: Alice only briefly mentions themed and gluten-free cakes, and no decisions seem to have been made yet. She does, however, state her preference for strawberries, so this is likely the answer.

Activity 2

1. C

Explanation: The sentences before and after the blank indicate that Sam has visited the driver's license website (diagram), but some details are unclear and he needs help.

2. B

Explanation: I know that Sam has a driver's license from another province, but it is no longer valid; by following the diagram, I can tell that he needs to visit his nearest Drive Ontario office.

3. A

Explanation: This blank likely still refers to the author's driver's license, which is no longer valid. According to the diagram, the author should visit the nearest Drive Ontario Office, but there is no mention of fees.

4. C

Explanation: Looking at the previous sentence, I understand that Sam's wife has a driver's license from a different province, and it is still valid. I look at the diagram and see that she has to fill out a form.

5. D

Explanation: Sam expresses how difficult he has found the website, and he doesn't think this is an information portal because not all the information he needs can be found on the website.

6. D

Explanation: Sam indicates that his wife has a valid driver's license from another province. By following the diagram, I can tell that she needs to fill out "License Exchange Form 55-2H." However, Sam also notes that he is having trouble finding this form. Therefore, the agent would likely include a link to this form in their response

Activity 3

1. E	3. B	5. C
2. D	4. A	

Activity 4

7.   D

Explanation: Sam did not find all of the information that he needed on the website. He is emailing to request more information.

- ✓ . . . please send us the required information.
- ✓ Subject: Questions
- ✓ . . . but some details are unclear to me.

Activity 5

1. Tone: disappointed
Clues: "I cannot believe" = shock, questioning; "failed" = disappointment
2. Tone: proud, excited
Clues: "congratulations," "!"
3. Tone: grateful
Clues: "appreciate"
4. Tone: ecstatic, excited
Clues: "best day," "thrilled"
5. Tone: sad, angry, or disappointed
Clues: "why," "hurtful"

Activity 6

8. A

Explanation: Sam is frustrated at the lack of information on this website.

- ✓ I would recommend this chart be updated soon . . .
- ✓ . . . but some details are unclear to me.
- ✓ It is difficult for me to view this as an "information portal," . . .

READING – UNIT 4

Activity 1

Topic: Informational interviews

Activity 2

| 1. A | 2. B | 3.C | 4. B |

Activity 3

- ✓ Informational interviews allow people to learn about a particular field.
- ✓ The purpose of informational interviews is to gather information.
- ✓ Employees share their view of the job, the environment, company, and qualifications with people interested in the field.

Activity 4

1. B

Explanation: The main idea of Paragraph B is getting ready for an informational interview, so this is where I'll start. I'm sure that "informed questions" is a key phrase in this statement, so I look for this phrase or a synonym in Paragraph B. I find the key words "research" and "asking questions" in Sentences 1 and 2. Sentence 2 is a paraphrase, so I choose "B."

2. E

Explanation: It's not clear which paragraph I should focus on. I eliminate Paragraph A because it's about how informational interviews are different from job interviews. The key word here is "resumé," and it could be mentioned in Paragraphs B, C, or D given the main ideas of those paragraphs. I scan the other three paragraphs for the word "resumé" or synonyms such as "curriculum vitae" or "CV." Since I'm a good scanner, I quickly see that the word "resumé" and likely synonyms aren't there. Therefore, I answer "E."

3. D

Explanation: The key words in this statement are "expectation" and "job offer," so I'll look for these in the text. I'll also look for synonyms such as "want" and "employment." I'm not sure which paragraph to start with, so I'll start at Paragraph A and work my way down. In Paragraph D, I see "job seeker should definitely not ask for employment"—this is a paraphrase of the statement, so "D" is correct.

4. A

Explanation: I see that this statement is a comparison, so I'll look for key words like "similar," "different," and "compare" in the text. I know that the main purpose of Paragraph A is to give a basic description of an informational interview, so I'll start there. I see "differ" in the second sentence, but it's discussing something else, so I'll move on. The bottom two sentences discuss job interviews and informational interviews respectively, describing the differences between the two. Therefore, A is the correct answer.

5. C

Explanation: This statement focuses on "appearance." I know that Paragraph C discusses how to present yourself in an informational interview, so this is likely the correct choice. In support of this, I see that the first sentence mentions "presentable attire." This is a synonym for an appropriate "appearance," so C is correct.

6. D

Explanation: I know that you "follow up" about something after the conclusion of an event. I remember that Paragraph D talks about the end of the informational interview, so I'll start there. A "courtesy" is a polite act, so I'll look for this word and its related synonyms (e.g., "gesture") in this paragraph. I see "nice gesture to send a short email" as well as "token of appreciation," therefore I know that D is correct.

7. E

Explanation: The key phrase here is "references," so I'll look for that, as well as its synonyms "contacts" and "former employer." I don't have any clear paragraph for this, so I'll start at the top. I quickly scan the message and see that none of these terms are present, therefore E is correct—the statement isn't present in any of the paragraphs.

8. C

Explanation: The key phrases in this statement are "personal contact," "beneficial," and "later." I'll look for these in the text, as well as synonyms like "connection," "good," and "future." I quickly scan the text from the top, and I see that Paragraph C discusses how "positive impressions" make "connections" easier in the "future." Therefore, C is correct.

9. E

Explanation: This statement focuses on "company," "sets up," and "job seeker's request." When I scan the text, I'll also look for synonyms like "employer," "start," and "ask for." I know that Paragraph A gives background about informational interviews, so I'll start there. I don't see anything about who sets up the interview here, so I'll move on to the next paragraph. Paragraphs B, C, and D don't mention this either, so the answer must be E—this statement isn't mentioned in any paragraph.

Activity 5A

1. J	4. A	7. H	10. B
2. G	5. K	8. D	11. F
3. L	6. C	9. E	12. I

Activity 5B

1. B	3. A	5. D
2. E	4. C	

Activity 6

PARAGRAPH A

Main Idea: The people who made the discovery
- 2012
- Fossil discovered
- Canadian Rockies
- Royal Ontario Museum
- University of Toronto

PARAGRAPH C

Main Idea: About *Siphusauctum gregarium*
- About 20 cm long
- Tulip-shaped body
- Small disc attaches to floor
- Lived on sea floor
- Found about 1,000

PARAGRAPH B

Main Idea: The Burgess Shale
- Has fossil remains of earliest animals
- Mostly soft-bodied, lived in oceans
- In Yoho National Park, BC
- 500 million years old

The rock was submerged then

PARAGRAPH D

Main Ideas: Importance of discovery OR What makes it unique
- Other discoveries are related to existing creatures
- *Siphusauctum gregarium* had a unique feeding system
- Fed on particles filtered from water
- Important discovery
- Shows animals then more diverse than we thought

Test Practice

1. A	4. D	7. B
2. C	5. C	8. E
3. E	6. E	9. D

READING – UNIT 5

Activity 1

1. Fact

Explanation: Even though the statistics in this sentence refer to the future, "reported" is used when stating facts. Therefore, this sentence is a fact.

2. Fact

Explanation: "Verify" is used when confirming a fact, and Lucinda Maxwell isn't introducing any opinion in this sentence; therefore, this sentence is a fact.

3. Fact

Explanation: The mayor is not expressing an opinion on anything; this is supported by the use of "state," which is typically used when describing facts. Therefore, this sentence is a fact.

4. Opinion

Explanation: The politicians are strongly suggesting that the government should take a certain action—nothing is definite yet. In addition, "assert" is a way of strongly indicating one's opinion; therefore, this is an opinion sentence.

5. Fact

Explanation: The article in this sentence is simply describing events in the past—no opinion is being offered. The verb "demonstrated" supports this. Therefore, this is a fact.

6. Fact

Explanation: "Disclose" is commonly used when offering facts about a situation. This is supported by the rest of the sentence, which describes events in the past. Therefore, this sentence expresses a fact.

7. Opinion

Explanation: "Argue" is a key indicator that what follows is an opinion. In this sentence, the mayor's critics are giving their opinion about his bike-friendly approach to traffic.

8. Fact

Explanation: "Realize" typically indicates that a person is learning a piece of information, not offering an opinion. This is supported by the rest of the sentence, where Lucinda Maxwell learns facts about other countries; therefore, this sentence expresses a fact.

9. Opinion

Explanation: The key word here is "believe"; this verb indicates that the environmentalists have no actual facts about the situation; instead, they are offering an opinion.

10. Opinion

Explanation: In this sentence, Gregor Robertson is giving his opinion about something that will occur in the future; he cannot prove this as fact. Moreover, "insisted" is commonly used when one is expressing a strong opinion.

11. Opinion

Explanation: The word "contends" indicates that Kelly Wong is giving her opinion on this topic.

12. Fact

Explanation: The subject of this sentence is "numbers"; since numbers can't offer opinions, this sentence is a fact. This is supported by the word "indicate," which is commonly used to state a fact.

Activity 2

1. C

Explanation: The use of the word "believes" identifies this statement as an expression of Robertson's opinion. In Line 7, you learn that "the city government insists that eliminating affordable parking zones will benefit the public." "Insists" is also a word that is used to express an opinion. As mayor, Robertson leads the city government, so you can conclude that he thinks the removal of "inexpensive parking spaces is good for the public."

2. A

Explanation: The word "assert" is used to express an opinion, so you should look in the text for a statement related to the car owners' opinion. In Line 5, "car owners contend that" higher parking costs are "unacceptable and unaffordable." Here, "contend" is also used to introduce an opinion. You can therefore conclude that car owners think they should have "access to affordable parking."

3. C

Explanation: The word "feel" is used to introduce the cyclists' opinion. The phrase "cyclists feel that" has a similar meaning to "cycling enthusiasts believe that," found in Line 10. If you look more closely at this part of the text, you can see that "there is no solution in sight yet for this disagreement" is a paraphrase of "there is no obvious resolution for this problem."

4. A

Explanation: Here the word "confirms" is a signal that this statement expresses a fact. In Lines 3-4, Robertson "stated that the city will be . . . raising the cost of residential parking permits by 750%." In this case, "stated" is used to introduce a fact. Option (a) summarizes this 750% increase by saying the cost of parking permits "will rise significantly for downtown residents."

Activity 3

The correct answer is (a): Population Growth: Should We Be Alarmed?

Activity 4

1. B

Explanation: Farzi's viewpoints are given in Paragraph 1, so focus your search here. Pay attention to negative words and phrases such as "raising fears," "exceed the carrying capacity," "rapid depletion of . . . resources," and "escalation in war, famine, . . ." Farzi is quoted in Sentence 3, saying that if the population keeps increasing, there will be too many people and not enough resources—which is a bad thing. Now look at your answer choices. Only one carries a strong negative meaning: "dismal." Since none of the other answers fit as well, this is your best choice.

2. C

Explanation: Gupta's views are explained in Paragraph 2. Everything he says reinforces his opinion that there are too many people in the world. Terms such as "above sustainable levels," "overpopulation," "limit population growth," and "catastrophe" communicate this viewpoint, and the answer is clearly given in Sentence 3: "We have to implement population control methods . . ." which is very close in meaning to answer (c). Note that the ideas in the other three answers are not mentioned in Paragraph 2.

3. C

Explanation: The first sentence of Paragraph 3 tells us that Kelly Wong's viewpoint will be very different from those of Farzi and Gupta, which implies that answers (a) and (d) can probably be eliminated. We learn in Sentence 2 that Wong feels population growth is slowing down, or "levelling off." Next, Wong talks about how fewer people now want to have children. This is the "changing values" in answer (c).

4. A

Explanation: Lucinda Maxwell's views are in Paragraph 4, so search here for the answer. A quick skim of this paragraph tells us that "consumption" is a key word, since it is used four times. "Consumption" and "consumed"—from answer (a)—are in the same word family, so answer (a) could be correct. Nothing comes up when you scan the paragraph for key ideas in the other three answers, which makes answer (a) more likely. Sentence 4 paraphrases answer (a), so that is the correct answer.

Activity 5

6. A	8. A	10. C
7. C	9. A	

Activity 6

1. Salt
2. Many people will find these clues extremely helpful:
   - ✓ grainy element
   - ✓ food consumption, food preservation
   - ✓ white granular substance
   - ✓ this seasoning found on most dining tables

   Some people may find these clues useful as well:
   - ✓ it has even been used as currency
   - ✓ essential to people
   - ✓ major revenue source

Activity 7

1. A	3. B	5. B
2. B	4. C	

Test Practice

1. D	4. C	7. A	10. D
2. B	5. D	8. D	
3. B	6. D	9. B	

WRITING – UNIT 7

Activity 1

GREETING	**Dear Building Manager,** **[LINE SPACE]**
OPENER	**I am writing to make a complaint about a problem that I am currently experiencing in apartment 214.** I'm sure you are aware of the no-dogs policy in the building. Over the last week I have heard a dog barking at various times throughout the day; however, it is loudest and most disturbing at night. I think that it sounds like the dog is in the apartment next door to mine. **[LINE SPACE, NEW PARAGRAPH]**
3 BODY PARAGRAPHS	If you could arrange to make a visit to the apartment during the daytime, I am sure you will see that there is a dog kept in the apartment, and then you could have a discussion with the renters about the dog's removal. **[LINE SPACE, NEW PARAGRAPH]**
CLOSER	I would be grateful for your action on this matter as soon as possible, as it is disrupting my sleep and my family's sleep as well. **If this problem isn't resolved soon, I'm afraid that I'll have to contact the local bylaw office.** **[LINE SPACE]**
SIGN-OFF	**Sincerely,**

Activity 2A

Negative Tone		Positive Tone	
Sarcastic	Aggressive	Respectful	Optimistic
Pessimistic	Critical	Helpful	Enthusiastic
Insulting	Angry	Co-operative	Understanding
Arrogant	Defensive	Complimentary	Sincere

Activity 2B

Email Component	Opener/Closer	Tone
Closer	1. Thank you in advance for dealing with this issue.	*Appropriate*
Opener	2. I am very sorry to bother you with a small problem related to a cute little dog.	*Inappropriate*
Opener	3. I have an issue that I'm hoping you can solve.	*Appropriate*
Closer	4. I request that you make sure this dog stops being a disturbance today.	*Inappropriate*
Closer	5. I expect to hear from you today with a satisfactory solution to this unbearable living situation.	*Inappropriate*

1. (Appropriate)

2. I am very sorry to bother you with a small problem related to a cute little dog.
Explanation: Unnecessary adjectives have been used in this sentence—"very," "small," "cute," and "little" are redundant here. Instead, you could say: "I am sorry to bother you about a problem related to a dog."

3. (Appropriate)

4. I request that you make sure this dog stops being a disturbance today.
Explanation: This sentence is too direct and negative. You could soften it like this: "Could you please make sure the dog is taken care of today?" Adding "please" here also makes the request sound politer and more appropriate.

5. I expect to hear from you today with a satisfactory solution to this unbearable living situation.
Explanation: This sentence is too direct and negative. You could make it less demanding and negative by saying: "I hope to hear from you today with a possible solution to this situation."

Activity 2C

1. C

Explanation: The writer has a request and wants the reader to speak with the tenant about his dog. (a) is too positive and (b) is too direct and demanding. (c) is the most appropriate.

2. B

Explanation: The writer has a request and wants the reader to deal with the problem. (a) is too assertive and direct. (c) sounds too demanding. The sentences need to be softer; therefore, (b) is the best option.

3. A

Explanation: (b) and (c) have used an overly negative tone to describe the dog. (a) has used an appropriate tone.

4. A

Explanation: The writer is expressing his interest in finding a solution to this problem. (b) is too direct and needs to be softened. (c) sounds too demanding. The best option to express his willingness in this matter is (a).

5. B

Explanation: The writer wants to express his appreciation in advance for the help he hopes to receive. Both (a) and (c) sound a bit demanding; (b) has the most appropriate tone.

6. A

Explanation: The writer wants to inform the reader of the pet policy in the building. (b) is too direct and needs to be softened. (c) is also too direct and is implying that the reader should have already learned about the pet policy.

Activity 3

1. C	2. B	3. C	4. B

Activity 4

1. A

Explanation: "Dear Mr. Jackson," is formal, but not overly formal. This is the standard Greeting for emails when we are writing to someone we don't know in a formal situation. "Hey Mr. Jackson," is too informal and almost disrespectful because of the colloquial term "Hey." "Respected Manager of 239 Oak Street," is overly formal and awkward, and would never be used by a native English speaker. "To Whom It May Concern," is cold and old-fashioned; most Canadians no longer use this expression unless they don't know the recipient and can't find any other appropriate Greeting.

2. D

Explanation: This answer is factual. The writer explains who he is and why he is writing, without being emotional or accusing. This is a good lead-in to an explanation of the problem and puts the reader in a receptive frame of mind. (a) is inappropriate because it is demanding ("you really must help me") and overstated ("unbearable problem"). (b) provides some useful information (by giving the street address) but the description of the problem leads the reader to question the credibility of the writer. "Massive hairy dog" is a somewhat ridiculous description, and how the dog looks isn't relevant. "Barks endlessly every single night" sounds like it is probably an exaggeration. (c) sounds desperate ("I have no idea what I'm going to do") and may cause the reader, again, to question the writer's credibility.

Activity 5A

	Greeting	Explanation
INF	Hey!	This is informal and would only be used between friends or people with whom you are very familiar. The use of an exclamation mark further supports this.
F	Dear Mr. Snow,	The combination of "Dear" and "Mr." would only be used in a formal situation.
B	Dear Jack,	Although "Dear" is commonly used in formal contexts, the use of the first name, "Jack," allows this greeting to be used in both formal and informal situations.
IA	Dude!	This is far too informal to be used in an email; it is inappropriate.
IA	Your Eminence,	This is far too formal to be used in an email; it is inappropriate.
F	To Whom It May Concern,	This is a formal greeting that might be used if you do not know the recipient's name.
	Body	**Explanation**
IA	You obviously don't care.	This statement is too accusatory; therefore, it is inappropriate.
B	I'd like to thank you.	The language here is quite neutral and could be used in both formal and informal contexts.
F	With respect to the aforementioned problem,	"With respect" and "aforementioned" are both very formal terms.
INF	And then there was the time	The language here (remembering a past event) is fairly informal and would probably only be used between friends or long-time acquaintances; therefore, it is informal.
F	I would like to draw your attention to	"I would" and "draw your attention" are commonly used in more formal situations.
B	Have you noticed that	The language here is quite neutral and could be used in both formal and informal contexts.
	Sign-off	**Explanation**
INF	TTYL	Abbreviations like this ("talk to you later") are commonly only used between friends; this is very informal.
B	Take care,	The language here is quite neutral and could be used in both formal and informal contexts.
INF	Hugs!	This term is informal and would only be used between friends or people with whom you are very familiar. The use of an exclamation mark further supports this.
F	Regards,	This sign-off is typically only used in formal situations.
F	Sincerely,	This sign-off is typically only used in formal situations.
IA	Yours most graciously,	This is far too formal to be used in an email; it is inappropriate.

Activity 5B

1. Hey!
2. Have you noticed that
3. TTYL
4. D
5. B
6. Angry, Critical

Please note that this is an example of a type of response you would not want to write on a test. The register is too informal and the tone is far too critical. This message will likely make the reader upset.

Activity 6

Purpose of Message	Suggest a general plan for the trip and ask for each team member's opinion.
Opener	I've been asked to organize our upcoming business trip to Toronto.
Point 1	1. Destination city 2. Business conference 3. Visit clients
Point 2	1. Dates away 2. Departure time 3. Arrival time
Point 3	1. Flight details 2. Hotel name and address
Point 4	1. Ask for each member's opinion 2. Give "reply by" date
Closer	Thank you in advance for your quick reply.

Activity 7

SAMPLE 1 (192 words)

Dear Team,

I am touching base with you in order to discuss our trip to Calgary at the beginning of next month to meet our colleagues at ABC Inc. The meeting has been scheduled from December 1 to December 4. I feel it is best to depart from YVR airport on the Tuesday evening after work. Our Air Canada flight leaves from Terminal 2 at 7:40 p.m. and arrives in Calgary at 10:15 p.m. local time. We have been booked into the Fairmont Hotel on Main Street, downtown Calgary, which is only a 5-minute walk from the offices of ABC Inc. Taxis will take us from the airport to the hotel.

Meetings will last the duration of Wednesday and Thursday. One set meal has been arranged with ABC on Wednesday evening at Cardero's restaurant beside the hotel. As for Thursday evening, if anyone has suggestions for dining or other activities, do let me know. We will have a brief meeting on Friday morning, before leaving for the airport to catch a 2:10 p.m. flight back to Vancouver.

Please advise if anyone has any suggestions they would like to add.

Kind regards,
Rory

SAMPLE 2 (201 words)

Hi Team,

After much investigation I have formulated a plan for our upcoming trip to Edmonton for the business conference. As we know, this runs from Tuesday, September 8th, until Thursday, September 10th, and we are scheduled to be on site from 9:00 a.m. to 5:00 p.m. every day.

Because of the early start and the distance to Edmonton, I have booked seats on a direct flight from Victoria to Edmonton on the evening of Monday, September 7th, leaving at 5:45 p.m. and arriving at 10:35 p.m. I would also like us to fly back on the night of Thursday, September 10th, and have made reservations on a 7:50 p.m. departure that gets us back into Victoria at 9:50 p.m. that night.

I have rooms on hold at the Fairmont in downtown Edmonton, as we have a long-standing business relationship with them, and the hotel is only a 10-minute cab ride from the conference. As well as this they provide a breakfast buffet from 6:30 a.m. every day and have an award-winning restaurant on site. Lunch is provided at the conference.

If anyone has any queries or suggestions about this plan, please do not hesitate to contact me.

Regards,

Greg Beazley

Activity 8

1. 4, 5, 7, 8, 11, 12
2. Travel times; Asking for their opinion
3. *Here is one way to fix the problems in this response. Note that the word count for this response is 163 words long.*

Dear Team Members,

As you are all aware, we will be travelling to Calgary this November for a series of meetings. I have been directed to take charge of the trip, so I am writing to share our travel plans and business goals.

We will be attending the annual meeting for residential realtors and meeting individually with four of the biggest Calgary real estate companies while we are there. We depart on November 24 at 5:50 p.m. on Westjet 719 and return on November 28, flying out at 8:30 a.m. and heading directly to the office upon our return.

In Calgary, we'll be staying downtown at the Palliser Hotel. This is one of the oldest buildings in the city and it's a four-star hotel, so we will be very comfortable and we'll be able to access local transportation very easily.

Please get back to me within a week and let me know how you feel about this plan.

With best wishes,

Jake Harkness

Activity 9A

1. B

Activity 9B

1. A
Explanation: The writer's original sentence essentially repeated the task instructions. Although this isn't incorrect, the writer could better demonstrate the range of his vocabulary by paraphrasing the situation like this.

2. C
Explanation: The writer's original sentence was quite repetitive; there is no need to repeat "watch" twice in the sentence. This version is more concise.

3. & 4. B
Explanation: In the original email, the writer repeated himself in the last two sentences. For more conciseness, these sentences could be combined. The addition of "phone or text me" also adds more detail.

Activity 10A

General Nouns	Specific Nouns/Noun Phrases	General Nouns	Specific Nouns/Noun Phrases
class	session fitness lesson weight training course meditation course	band	watch band watch strap
watch	timepiece wristwatch	gym	fitness centre leisure centre health club
area	studio change room practice space	person	grandparent grandmother grandfather

Activity 10B

Common Adjectives	Descriptive Adjectives/Adjective Phrases	Common Adjectives	Descriptive Adjectives/Adjective Phrases
red	deep crimson scarlet ruby	important	highly significant essential of great consequence
lost	nowhere to be found completely vanished missing	last	final after everything else in the end
expensive	very costly pricey high-priced	sad	thoroughly miserable truly unhappy gloomy

Activity 10C

Weak Verbs	Strong Verbs/Verb Phrases	Weak Verbs	Strong Verbs/Verb Phrases
lose	misplace completely lose track of be unable to find	think	believe suppose assume
find	come across get back retrieve	get	get a hold of obtain
call	get in touch with give me a call phone me	have	have in my possession own

Activity 11

1. took a spin class
2. I realized right away
3. I had somehow forgotten
4. stow it safely away
5. hot yoga studio
6. is hidden away
7. has great sentimental value
8. final gift
9. I'll be visiting
10. next week
11. As I hope you can see
12. contact me as soon as you possibly can

Activity 12

First in a series of actions		Last in a series of actions	
to begin with first	first of all firstly	finally lastly	in the end ultimately
Actions happening at the same time		**Action that comes after another action**	
meanwhile when	during while	after that then	after next
Actions at a specific time		**Unexpected action**	
at 2:00 (clock time) in 2 weeks (number of minutes, days, weeks, months, years)	next year (or week or month) 3 hours later	suddenly unexpectedly	without warning all of a sudden

Activity 13

1. to begin with
2. at 2:00 p.m.
3. after
4. next
5. meanwhile
6. the next morning
7. before
8. suddenly

Activity 14A

1. E
2. G
3. B
4. F
5. A
6. D
7. C

Activity 14B

1. ✗
2. ✓
3. ✓
4. ✗
5. ✗
6. ✓
7. ✓
8. ✓

Activity 15

1. because
2. For instance,
3. so that
4. Although
5. In order to
6. As well as
7. Similarly,
8. If

Activity 16

1. C

Explanation: There are a number of clear capitalization and punctuation errors here, including lowercased letters at the beginnings of sentences, and incorrect end punctuation for sentences.

D

Explanation: This response contains a run-on sentence, as well as some fragments and short sentences that could be improved by expanding them or joining them to longer sentences.

2. A

Explanation: Some readers may find ". . . I have a problem with your building." too direct/assertive. It could be improved by adding more detail and formal language. For example, ". . . I am writing about a problem I've been experiencing in my apartment in the hope that you can help me resolve the situation."

C

Explanation: In addition to being too direct, "how come" is also too informal. This statement could be improved like this: "Why is it that this neighbour owns a dog in an apartment building with a clear no-dog policy?"

3. All corrections are shown in blue.

Good day,

I am **John**, one of your tenants, and I have a problem with your building. Every evening when **I** am relaxing, watching television, or eating my dinner, I **hear** a dog barking in the next apartment. This is distracting, especially at night when **I** am sleeping. **I** am writing you an email **because** I do not want my neighbours to get mad at me when I talk to them about their dog. Could you speak to the tenants in the next apartment about this, and remind them that dogs are not allowed in the building?

I wonder how a dog owner ended up living here, since this building has **a** no-dog policy? **How** come one of my neighbours has one? Please understand **I'm** not a dog hater. **I** just want some real privacy and silence at night.

Can you visit my **neighbour tomorrow** and explain that dogs aren't allowed in the building? Maybe you can help them decide what to do about their dog.

Hoping for your kind actions,

John Parkdale

Although further changes could be made to this response, for more consistent tone and additional detail, only the clear grammar and punctuation mistakes are shown here. These types of mistakes are often the easiest to identify and correct as you're checking your work near the end of your response time.

Activity 17

This version has been revised to include basic formatting and paragraphing corrections. It is 192 words long.

Dear Sir,
[**LINE SPACE**]
Having moved into your building recently, I was under the impression that there was a no-dogs rule.
[**LINE SPACE, NEW PARAGRAPH**]
However, each evening I can hear a dog barking in the next apartment and I am write to ask for your help with this. This is ridiculously unacceptable. Some nights I am awakened at 2:00 a.m. by the barking, and I find it challenging to focus at work the next day.
[**LINE SPACE, NEW PARAGRAPH**]
I am a doctor, it is important that I am always at my best for my patients. This building is near to my work, and also chose it specifically for the no-dogs rule, as I had problems in my previous apartment with dog noise. My badly sleeping was beginning to affect my work, and now the situation isn't any better since I'm having the same problems.
[**LINE SPACE, NEW PARAGRAPH**]
I know dogs are part of people's family, but would like you to sort out this problem. I'm not looking for a rent decrease. As this would not resolve the situation, but maybe I could move to another apartment away from the noise, or the person next door could move to another apartment.
[**LINE SPACE**]
Sincerely,
[**LINE SPACE**]
Raji Hundai

This second version has been revised to include better wording, grammar, and a more appropriate tone. It is now 199 words long.

Dear Sir,

Having moved into your building recently, I was under the impression that there was a no-dogs rule.

However, each evening I can hear a dog barking in the next apartment and I am **writing** to ask for your help with this. This is **a very difficult situation for me**. Some nights I am awakened at 2:00 a.m. by the barking, and I find it challenging to focus at work the next day.

Since I am a doctor, it is important that I am always at my best for my patients. This building is near to my work, and **I** also chose it specifically for the no-dogs rule, as I had problems in my previous apartment with dog noise. My **poor sleep** was beginning to affect my work, and now the situation isn't any better since I'm having the same problems.

I know dogs are part of people's **families**, but **I** would like you to sort out this problem. I'm not looking for a rent decrease, **as** this would not resolve the situation, but maybe I could move to another apartment away from the noise, or the person next door could move to another apartment.

Sincerely,

Raji Hundai

WRITING – UNIT 8

Activity 1

#	Steps to complete Task 2
6	Write and organize your response.
3	Scan the right side for specific information about the task and the two options.
4	Quickly decide which option you will write about.
2	Scan the left side to find the role, audience, and situation for the task.
5	Quickly create an outline.
1	Skim the instructions to get a general idea of what you need to do.
7	Edit and improve your response.

Activity 2

   1. A   2. B   3. A   4. A

Activity 3

- ✓ She wrote as an employee at a big store.
  Explanation: She writes "Thank you, manager, for the discount," and this tells us that she is an employee at a store.
- ✓ She wrote to her employer.
  Explanation: Again, her use of the word "manager" in the first sentence tells us who she is writing to. Note: addressing a specific person is acceptable in this case; however, depending on the task instructions, you won't always need to do this.
- ✓ She made a choice between the two options.
  Explanation: She doesn't talk about the other option, but she clearly states which discount she wants.
- ○ She explained her choice.
  Explanation: This writer does not provide a convincing explanation because she gives us only one reason, and that is not enough.
- ○ She gave several reasons for her choice.
  Explanation: This writer gives just one reason for her choice, which is that she wants to buy furniture for her house. All the details provide support for this one reason, but the details are simply a shopping list.
- ○ She wrote 150–200 words.
  Explanation: She writes just 130 words.

Activity 4

1. *There are many possible answers. Here are some examples.*

	OPTION A: I prefer a 20% discount on all products, not including groceries.	OPTION B: I prefer a 10% discount on all products, including groceries.
Supporting Reasons	• Excellent savings • Makes many things affordable • Benefits homeowners making major purchases • Supports employees in improving quality of life	• Benefits most employees since many of us buy our groceries here • Reduces cost of living for those buying groceries here • Makes groceries more affordable • Employees' families benefit regularly
Reason Against	• Food essentials won't be as affordable	• Larger discount on other items would be appreciated
Vocabulary	• Greater savings • Household items • Homeowners • Not food-oriented • Clothing	• Daily needs • One-stop shopping • Struggling to make ends meet • Equitable • Necessities of life

2. The number of reasons you find to support each option will vary. You may end up choosing Option B because it can be difficult to come up with good reasons supporting a discount that doesn't include groceries. Everyone needs to buy groceries.

Activity 5

1.
✓ It's totally obvious that every single employee of this company will be forever grateful . . .
✓ It would be idiotic . . .
✓ Honestly, who can imagine . . .

2. A

Activity 6

1. *There are many ways to complete this chart. Here is one example.*

	OPTION A: Replace parking spaces on one side of the street with a bike lane	OPTION B: Keep parking spaces on both sides of the street
Supporting Reasons	• Many houses have garages, driveways • Paved areas can be used for parking • Makes cycling safer for cyclists • Encourages people to use transit instead of cars	• Will reduce congestion and traffic jams • Most families have two or three cars • Reduces double-parking incidents • Increases revenues since we can charge for parking
Reason Against	• Residents want extra parking for visitors	• No bike lanes causes accidents for cyclists
Vocabulary	• resident convenience • out of necessity • demographics • safety measures	• double parking • traffic congestion • parking revenue • cycling accidents

Test Practice

OPTION A

This Level 12 response is 196 words long.

As an avid cyclist and a long-time resident of this neighbourhood, I think a bike lane makes a lot of sense for our streets.

First of all, most houses in the neighbourhood have their own garages and driveways which offer plenty of parking. Most residents park on the street for convenience, not out of necessity. There are also plenty of paved, unused spaces which could be better utilized as parking lots. Charlotte Street and Morgan Street are already frequently used by cyclists in order to avoid traffic on main roads. And parking on both sides combined with the absence of bike lanes has already caused a few accidents to cyclists.

Second, the resident demographic is changing, as a lot of young professionals are drawn to the old architectural charm our neighbourhood offers. Most of them commute by bicycle, and the streets are already proving perilous for them. So, taking into account the evolving demographic in the area, and the fact that cyclists are already using these streets despite the lack of bike lanes, I think the city should take measures toward their safety by adding bike lanes. I hope my opinion will be considered. Thank you.

OPTION B
This Level 12 response is 191 words long.

While I do sympathize with the cyclists' position of seeking to attain a bike lane as an avid cyclist myself, I would still prefer to keep the current parking arrangements. As it is now, there are currently no other parking alternatives in the immediate vicinity, as the closest available parking is at least a mile away. Therefore, unless the government is willing to demolish an existing structure to erect a parking facility to accommodate the motoring public, then I would strongly urge them to leave the existing parking arrangements in place. In addition, it should be noted that the existing parking arrangement is insufficient, as each household is only permitted parking for one vehicle. Therefore, with this constraint in mind it would be extremely difficult on the motoring public if there were further parking restrictions.

If I may, I would like to suggest to the government that instead of disrupting the current parking situation, that they should instead reserve 4 feet from the end of the right parking lane for the cyclists. This would satisfy both the motoring public that needs parking and the cyclists that need safer means of commuting.

Activity 7

1. From my perspective,
   I think
2. . . . exchange parking spaces for a bike lane on all the streets in our neighbourhood.
   . . . replace parking spaces on one side of the street with a bike lane.

Activity 8

Here are some ideas you could use to support this opinion:
OPINION: "Pay $1 each time I have tea or coffee."
SUPPORTING IDEAS:
- This plan reduces trash because people are likely to waste the drinks if they are free.
- The other option encourages over-consumption of caffeine, which is bad for our health.
- The other option may result in employees spending too much time in the coffee room and not enough time working.
- Different employees drink different amounts of coffee and tea, so this is the only fair way.
- I have only a few hot drinks per week, so this is more affordable.
- Most employees here prefer cold drinks.
- One dollar is a very fair price.
- One dollar is much less than we would pay at a coffee shop.

Activity 9

Here is one example of how you could choose and develop your ideas:
OPINION: "Pay $1 each time I have tea or coffee."
POINT 1: THE OTHER OPTION ENCOURAGES OVER-CONSUMPTION OF CAFFEINE
- People would feel free to have numerous cups each day.
- This would result in too much caffeine for some people.
- Drinking too much caffeine could have a negative impact on some employees' health, social interactions, and work productivity.

POINT 2: DIFFERENT EMPLOYEES DRINK DIFFERENT AMOUNTS OF COFFEE AND TEA
- Some people will benefit, but others will lose money.
- This could create antagonism amongst the staff.
- It's not a fair plan for everyone.

POINT 3: I HAVE ONLY A FEW HOT DRINKS A WEEK
- I'll be spending $2–$3 per week.
- I'll save money.
- Other employees who don't enjoy hot drinks will also save money.

Test Practice

OPTION A

This sample Level 12 response is 192 words long.

I think paying $15 per month for unlimited hot beverages is clearly a better option. Dividing the cost equally among employees fosters a sense of community and encourages participation, which has the indirect benefit of increased socialization—a longstanding tradition, a community-building experience, and a recognized factor in workplace productivity.

Paying $1 per drink assesses an increasingly stringent penalty for frequent use, which discourages use of the service. An unfortunate byproduct of such a plan could be reduced socialization, the benefits of which I've already discussed. As such I fear that the second option could remove the need for a "hot drinks" service altogether.

My choice is also motivated by arithmetic, though. I feel I should state this explicitly. A standard month is thirty days with four weekends and one holiday, for twenty-one total business days. The first plan costs less than the second if each employee consumes one hot drink per working day. Now consider that Edmonton's winter temperatures remain at -20°C for weeks, and below 0°C for six months of a typical year. Given our climate, I suspect most employees drink more hot beverages than that. I know I do.

OPTION B

This sample Level 12 response is 178 words long.

In relation to the recent survey that has been circulated about the tea and coffee payment policy, I wish to pay $1 per hot drink. My reason is that I imagine it will encourage me to be more aware of just how much caffeine I am consuming in the workplace. Also, I believe that I will be more economically sensible with this option as opposed to choosing to pay $15 a month.

I have found that in situations where I am granted unlimited tea and coffee, my inner caffeine addict comes to the fore and I begin to border on unhealthy daily doses! Paying a dollar a drink will serve as a means to discipline myself in this regard as it really is unnecessary to drink so much caffeine. Besides, if the urge really does take me, a more economically viable solution would be for me to bring my own flask of tea from home in the mornings.

I appreciate being asked for my preference on this matter. I look forward to a healthier future with the company!

Activity 10

1. **Since** most employees drink two coffees a day **and** work five days per week, **it follows that** they pay $10 per week for coffee.
2. I would like to pay $15 per month **because** it's more convenient **than** paying with cash.
3. It can be irritating to pay each time; **as a result**, we may be distracted from our work **when** we're worrying about having cash.
4. This will reduce my coffee expenses, **which** will help me save money **because** I consume a lot of coffee every day.
5. **By** making coffee and tea affordable, this plan increases social interaction for the staff **and results in** happier employees.

Activity 11

1. to start with
2. that
3. because
4. similarly
5. consequently/as a result
6. another
7. although
8. as a result/consequently
9. when
10. for example

Activity 12

1. a) YES. See Paragraph 1, Sentence 2.
   b) YES. I explain that I want Option A so I can buy food for my large family (Paragraph 1), and then I write about the cost of groceries (Paragraph 2). However, since my two reasons are somewhat related, I wasn't able to separate them as effectively as I would have liked.
   c) YES. Each reason includes several good supporting details.

2. "No" answers for the following: #3, #4, #7, #8, and #9
   #3. When stating his preference at the beginning, this test taker copies directly from the prompt. After that, he uses the same key words repeatedly (choose, food, family, bill, products) without rephrasing them.
   #4. See the explanation for #3. This writer should have tried to find more precise words when repeating key ideas.
   #7. There are too many simple sentences in this response.
   #8. The salutation and sign-off are much too informal for this situation. In addition, the last sentence seems rude and would benefit from adding "please" before "give me."
   #9. There are many places in this response where the writer could have used joining words to create longer sentences and improve coherence.

Activity 13

1. D
VOCABULARY: This writer has an impressive vocabulary range and she rephrases ideas with ease. Some examples of good word choice include "higher cost," "lower percentage," "a reasonable amount," "an annual profit," and "continued purchasing."
SENTENCE VARIETY: There is a nice variety of sentence types and lengths. However, there are some issues with sentence structure that should have been fixed.
TONE AND REGISTER: This writer is using an appropriately factual tone and a formal register.
Here is one suggested version to improve this response. This response is now 178 words long and could probably earn a Level 8–9 instead of a Level 7.

I would prefer the 10% option as I do all my shopping **over the year**, including groceries, ~~over the year at yours~~ company.
[**LINE SPACE, NEW PARAGRAPH**]
Working it out over a 12-month period, ~~for me to take if I took~~ the 20% discount, which does not include groceries, ~~would mean that~~ I would ~~either~~ be purchasing my groceries from another store at a higher cost ~~to myself. Which when you think~~ If I accept the lower percentage on all products including groceries, I would be saving quite a reasonable amount financially, and ~~that~~ your company would still be making an annual profit through my continued purchasing within the store.
[**LINE SPACE, NEW PARAGRAPH**]
I feel it is better for both you as a company and myself as a customer to have a smaller percentage over the whole range of products **rather** than a higher percentage on all products except groceries. **If all your employees take advantage of this offer, your company will certainly benefit from increased sales. Given that you employ hundreds of people, this should significantly increase the company's revenue, resulting in both happy employees and happy management.**
[**LINE SPACE, NEW PARAGRAPH**]
I look forward to a **productive** customer-employer bond that will continue for many years.